The March for Justice
(The Montgomery Bus Boycott)

by
Dorothy Swygert

for
Dramatic Production

Sections of this publication were reprinted by
arrangement with INTELLECTUAL PROPERTIES
MANAGEMENT, ATLANTA, GEORGIA, AS EX-
CLUSIVE LICENSOR OF THE KING ESTATE
Published by Rekindling the Heart, Inc.
P.O. Box 130360
Jamaica, New York 11413
Manufactured in the United States of America

ISBN 0-9648737-0-2

Library of Congress Catalog Card No: 127-684

THE MARCH FOR JUSTICE
(The Montgomery Bus Boycott)

by
Dorothy Swygert

Keeping the Dream Alive
Drama: The Montgomery Bus Boycott
Educational Resources for all levels
Golden Literary Treasury

Rekindling the Heart, Inc
New York

Table of Contents

Introduction   vii
Acknowledgments   xi
(Drama Showcase)
    The March for Justice: The Montgomery
        Bus Boycott   1
The Golden Literary Treasury   **21**
    The Day of Days, December 5   23
        Dr. Martin Luther King
    April 16, 1963: Letter From
        Birmingham Jail   35
        Dr. Martin Luther King
    I Have A Dream   55
        Dr. Martin L. King
    The Legacy of Martin L. King, Jr.   65
        Coretta Scott King
    The Courage to Live Life to the Fullest   69
        Dr. Martin L. King
Important Dates in the Life of
Dr. Martin L. King, Jr.   **71**
Educational Resources for Golden
    Literary Treasury   **79**

ADDENDUM   **89**

Suggested Classroom Activities for The
    Montgomery Bus Boycott   91
Conyers' King Bill Wins After 15 Years   97
Reading List   101
Films and Audio Visual Aids   107

Dedicated to the children
throughout the land
in search of obtaining
a global peace

INTRODUCTION

As a native of Alabama, I grew up in Fairfield, suburbs of Birmingham. The 1950's was such a decade of vigor and excitement. I am sure that I was quite fortunate to be an eyewitness to the bursting of seams of history in the "great state of Alabama." By 1955, one of the greatest changes since slavery was coming forth in my time to radicalize life in the South.

Since the days of Reconstruction, black people in Alabama had accepted and obeyed the segregated laws of this state. The doctrine of separate and equal was applied to all social customs in this part of the nation. A traveler, walking through, could easily observe the signs and witness the accepted behavior of second-class-citizenship. There were separate bathrooms, water fountains, no service at lunch counters, no admission to public parks, exclusion from public libraries, and designated seating for blacks—in the back of the bus!

During December, the busiest month of the shopping year, in the year of 1955, black people in Montgomery, under the leadership of a young black preacher, staged a **BUS BOYCOTT.** Through the years, black people had not only been humiliated by second-class-citizenship, but had suffered physical abuse. There were cases where some had lost their lives in trying to obtain the dignity of being a human being. In response to the mistreatment of **ROSA PARKS,** MEMBERS OF THE BLACK COMMUNITY QUICKLY ORGANIZED. The Montgomery Bus Boycott under the direction of Dr. Martin Luther King, Jr. remained in force for 381 days, until blacks had won their rights and demands. On December 21, 1956, the buses in Alabama were operating on a "First come, first served basis!" After this great feat, Dr. King became a household name throughout the state of Alabama.

I was inspired to write this play, **The March for Justice** (The Montgomery Bus Boycott), for my students in the New York City school system. As a social studies teacher, I would encourage my students to read past history and to keep abreast to current history. I had been exposed to the work of Dr. King in my home state. In 1963, I came home from college during the Easter vacation to find almost a ghost town. The usual shopping for the holidays was at a stand still. Dr. King was in jail and all the people had joined in the boycott, students, neighbors and all were locked in jail with him. For me, this impression remained in my mind. It is no wonder that I have sought to keep The King's Dream alive. The echo of his address at my Commencement at Tuskegee remains close to my heart.

In 1974, I involved a seventh grade reading class in fulfilling the request of William Harris, Principal of Linden Junior High School in Queens, New York for the observance of Black History Month. Mr. Harris, a Virginian, who was concerned about the total development of the children never ceased to implement programs that would nurture them in their history and culture, inspire them to work to their fullest potential and encourage them to glow with a sense of pride in realizing the rewards of their gifts and talents. These students were so excited about this assignment until they memorized and dramatized this play within a two and one-half-week period. The presentation was a showcase performance in celebration of a Black History Month. Our beloved principal, Mr. William Harris, was in awe as he sat with Mr. Howard Rubenstein, Superintendent in District 29, during that year.

Since that time, this play has been performed by junior and senior high school students, churches and high school staff.

The March for Justice (The Montgomery Bus Boycott) is almost a magic play. No matter where the play is performed it "comes off as a success."

As a historian, I would like to continue to share a legacy of the past with our children of the future. Who knows where the next leaders may be born to move us closer to a more right and just democratic nation.

Acknowledgments

The March for Justice (The Montgomery Bus Boycott) would not have become a reality without the assistance of many people who helped to make it a success. This play has been a dream to me. It is short enough to be performed in a regular school assembly program and flexible enough to be expanded. The uniqueness of this play is that one does not have to be an expert drama teacher to direct a performance. This play can come alive through the hands of a regular classroom teacher or any interested person. There is a kind of joy that captures the participants and audience in the preparation and the performance of this play.

I would like to express sincere appreciation to some individuals, schools, community centers, churches and staff members who have already participated in helping to keep the King's Dream alive. I salute District 29, where the play originated in Linden Junior High School in Queens. Ms. Celestine Miller is the current superintendent of this district and is carrying out the tradition of providing historical and cultural programs to enrich the lives of these students.

I am grateful to the retired principal of Andrew Jackson High School, Murray Bromberg, who was so enthusiastic about the performance of this play in 1979. Some of his students participated in the Delta Sigma Theta Sorority salute to Black Heritage Month at the St. Thomas Moore Church in Queens.

This play has been performed in Concord Baptist Church in Brooklyn with children and teachers of the Sunday School. I extend my appreciation to Karamoko Andrews, Samori Swygert, Shomari Andrews, Shana Williams, and other Sunday School students, who played leading roles in performing this play at Concord Baptist Church. The Saint Albans Family Life Center (Herbert Ross Johnson) in Jamaica, Queens brought a true revelation to me. As I worked in the After School Center with early school age children (grades one through four), I experienced such a joy in reducing the content for this level. I was truly amazed with these students. They gave a "Class A" performance before a full adult audience. I guess this is one reason why I refer to this play as a magic play.

The March for Justice (The Montgomery Bus Boycott) has been performed on elementary, junior high and senior high school levels. It has been widely accepted in churches and community centers. In January 1996, the Chaplain Interns, under the supervision of Chaplain George West, in a commemorative program for Dr. Martin L. King, performed this play at the New York Hospital Medical Center of Queens. I am grateful to the Chaplain Interns: Rosanna Ciavarella, Derrick Thompson, Samuel Sampson, Fidel Cossock, and Christopher Ponnuraj.

My most memorable moments in the production of this play took place in 1995 in August Martin

High School in Queens with staff members. The students were pleasantly surprised and overjoyed in observing their teachers as performers: Lennie Berg, Renee R. Calhoun, Celia Foster, Bob Gross, Norman Hocker, Kevin Jenkins, Adream Matthews, Dennis Menger, Craig Stevens, Naomi Stonehill with Patricia Singletary, Debbie Summers and Eleanor Allert as stage managers.

I am grateful to Mary R. Grant, an inspiring colleague whom I met in my first years of teaching in New York City. She is an energetic person who has always displayed a great love in teaching the children in this city. She has not only been an inspiration to me but an inspiration to the children and the community. I extend thanks to her for providing me with the opportunity to produce a new version of the play. In 1990, when she served as Executive Director of the St. Albans Family Life Center (Herbert Ross Johnson), I was the director for the After School Program. While working with the younger children, I was overjoyed at the presentation made by these children in grades one through four. I am further grateful to Mary R. Grant for providing the typing services for my first publication of this play under the title, The Montgomery Bus Boycott.

I extent profound appreciation to Terisa Ragin, Veronica Johnson Steward, Rose Ross, Ruby Yates, Doris Rutledge and Omar Swygert for reading and critiquing the play.

Without any further ado, I offer this play to you with a tender sense of joy to humankind in hopes that each one of us will play a greater role in helping to fully realize the dream of Dr. Martin L. King as we seek to make this a more just society.

Rosa Parks

The March for Justice

(The Montgomery Bus Boycott)
by Dorothy Swygert

<u>CHARACTERS</u>

Narrator	Sister Grace
Rosa Parks	Old Lady
Policeman	Annie Lou
Bus Driver	Mary Lucy
Taxi Driver	Sister Ann
Martin L. King, Jr.	Reporter/Secretary
Ralph D. Abernathy	Leona Mason
Helen Peterson	Charles Bowman
Raymond Willis	Claudette Williams
Paul Hardy	Jo Ann Wilson
White Man	Old Man

(Two or more roles may be played by one person.)

<u>ACT I</u>

SCENE 1: December 1, 1955

NARRATOR: Place: Court Square in Montgomery, Alabama.

Public bus—whites are seated in the front and blacks are seated in the back. The Cleveland Avenue Bus stops at Court Square. A tired, attractive black woman enters the bus. She moves to the back of the bus to the designated section for black people. She was lucky! There was just one seat left in this section. The black woman walked to the fifth row of the bus and sat next to a Black man.

Rosa Parks: (Enters crowded bus and sit down wearily).

NARRATOR: The bus driver's next stop is at the Empire Theater. Several white people boarded the bus. One white man could not find a seat.

Bus Driver: (Looks in rear view mirror) "Get up and give this man a seat!"

NARRATOR: The four black people who sat in the fifth row did not respond. This was certainly an unusual day. For years, black people had obeyed the segregated laws without the slightest amount of resistance.

Bus Driver: "Y'all better make it light on your-
selves and let me have those seats."
(A black man crosses over Rosa
Parks to relinquish his seat).

Rosa Parks: (Moves into the seat next to the
window—two   Black   women
across the aisle vacate their seats—
Rosa remains in her seat).

White Man: "Bus driver, will you ask this black
woman to get up and give me this
seat!"

Bus Driver: (Stops the bus—approaches Rosa.)
Let me have that seat!"

Rosa Parks: "No!"

Bus Driver   "Let me have that seat or else I will
call the police!"

Rosa Parks: (Shrugs her shoulders in a negative manner and still refuses to
give up her seat).

"Go ahead and call them."

Bus Driver: (Storms to the front of the bus and
pulls the ratchet—leaves the bus to
call the police).

NARRATOR: J. F. Blake, the bus driver returned
with two policemen.

Policemen: (Rosa Parks was approached by
two policemen).

"Will you get up and give your seat
to the man?"

Rosa Parks: "Why do you push us around?"

Policemen: "I don't know, but the law is the law and you are under arrest!"

(Policeman snatches Rosa by the arm and remove her from the bus).

NARRATOR: For the crime of not giving up her seat to a white man, Mrs. Rosa Parks, a respected member of the black community, was taken to jail. There she was booked and finger-printed. She was charged with violating the City's segregation law. During the past year alone, five black women and two black children had been arrested for disobeying bus drivers. One man had been shot to death by a policeman for the same offense.

Mrs. Parks had served as secretary of the local branch of the NAACP. Mr. E. D. Nixon, head of the NAACP, heard of her arrest and quickly posted bail for her release. She was later convicted and fined $10.00 and cost—a total of $14.00. The arrest of Rosa Parks triggered the Montgomery Bus Boycott. News of her arrest spread quickly through the black community like wild fire.

SCENE 2: **ORGANIZATION OF THE BOY-COTT AND M.I.A. (MONT-GOMERY IMPROVEMENT ASSOCIATION)**

Meeting: (Angry crowd of blacks, walking around humming, buzzing and talking).

Mrs. Mason: "You know they took our neighbor, Mrs. Rosa Parks to jail because she wouldn't give her seat to a white man!

Mrs. Peterson: "Shō nice black sister—I hate that!"

Mr. Bowman: "Just plain refused to give up her seat—she show got some guts in her trough!"

Mr. Willis: "I don't blame her—we're tired of our women being treated like they are some working horses."

Crowd: "Amen! Amen! tell it like it is."

Mr. Hardy: "And I feel that if we pay our money to ride on a public bus, we should be able to keep our seats."

Mrs. Wilson: "I'm tired of giving up my seat to a white person after I've paid my money."

Dr. King: (appears before the crowd).

"I've got a plan! I said, Black people, I have a Plan!"

Mr. Willis: "Who are you?"

Dr. King: "I'm Martin Luther King, Jr. and I am concerned about what's going on today with our people. I don't think that Black people ought to continue to accept segregation and second-class-citizenship. I think we, as a people, can make a change in these segregated laws."

Mrs. Mason: "Just how do you figure we can do that? We've been segregated for more than a hundred years!"

Crowd: "Yeah, what kind of plan do you have?"

Mr. Bowman: "I say, let's hear the plan!"

Dr. King: "My brothers and sisters—this evening, I want to tell you that there is nothing like, UNITY,—We've got to have some, TOGETH-ERNESS,—then we can really organize a boycott, against the buses in Montgomery, Alabama!"

Sister Grace: "What do you mean?"

Dr. King: "I mean, DON'T RIDE THE BUSES!"

Mr. Willis: "Just how do you figure I'm gonna get to work?

Annie Lou: "I've got to get to church!"

Sister Ann: "And I got to go shopping!"

Dr. King: "I am aware of your needs. We can organize to help ourselves. We can form car pools. People who own cars will share their cars.

Mr. Hardy: "Do you think that this will really work?"

Dr. King: "Do you own a car?"

Mr. Hardy: "Yeah!"

Dr. King: "Are you willing to share your car for the cause?"

Mr. Bowman: "I will!"

Mrs. Williams: "My brother has a car—I'm sure he will share it!"

Taxi Driver: "I'm a taxi driver and I believe I can persuade some of the other Black taxi drivers to lend you a hand. There are 18 Black taxi stands with a total of 210 cars."

Dr. King: "This is, indeed, a good showing this evening. Most of you know Rev. Abernathy, Pastor of the First Baptist Church in this city. He will read to you a list of resolutions which we will present to the bus and city officials. Come forward, Rev. Abernathy!"

Rev. Abernathy: (The two men shake hands— group applaud.)

"We are involved in a very important cause. There is a need for us to take a stand. This is the time for us to let white people know that we are not going to accept this second-class treatment. Brothers and sisters, we have a very important duty to perform! I say to you that we must unite for this cause. I have, here, a list of demands to be met before we end our boycott:

1) Black people will not ride the buses until a more courteous treatment by bus drivers is guaranteed!

2) All passengers are to be seated on a "first come, first served basis."

Crowd: "Amen—that's right—we want equal rights."

3) We want black people from the back of the bus and white people from the front of the bus."

Crowd: "Praise God—That's the truth!"

4) We want Black bus drivers employed to drive largely black routes."

Dr. King: "Thank you Rev. Abernathy. All those who are ready to accept these demands will you please stand!"

Crowd: (The majority stand—two or three sit for a few seconds, then stand).

Dr. King: "Just for the spirit of UNITY, I would like everyone to repeat after me:

(The crowd will repeat the words after Dr. King)

I WILL NOT RIDE, THE PUBLIC BUSES, IN MONTGOMERY, ALABAMA, UNTIL THEY ARE, DESEGREGATED, AND THAT ALL PEOPLE, BLACK AND WHITE, ARE TREATED, ON A FIRST COME, FIRST SERVE BASIS."

Dr. King: "Let us all join in and sing, 'We shall Overcome,' as we march out tonight."

NARRATOR: Instead of riding the buses, Black people thumbed rides; shared their cars, rode mules, and some middle aged people even walked as much as twelve (12) miles a day to keep from riding the bus. When Black people learned that Mrs. Rosa Parks had been found guilty of disobeying the segregation law and fined $14.00—this gave them a greater incentive to boycott the buses.

THE BOYCOTT

(Crowd carry placards: "DON'T RIDE THE BUSES," "FIRST

COME, FIRST SERVED," "END SEGREGATION," "DON'T DIS- CRIMINATE," "FIRST-CLASS CITIZENSHIP NOW," and "RE- MEMBER ROSA PARKS"!)

(The boycotters march around two times before stopping for the first speaker. Each speaker moves to centermost stage, holds up placard and speaks with authority. The en- tire group of boycotters stop to at- tention for each speaker and then resume the circle).

Dr. King: (Holds up placard and stops with a firm stand and speaks in an au- thoritative voice)

"Don't ride the buses!"

Rev. Abernathy: (Holds up placard and speaks in a demanding tone)

"First come, first served!"

Boycotter #3:   (Holds up placard and speaks in an assertive tone)

"End segregation, now!"

Boycotter #4:   (Holds up placard and speaks in a warning tone)

"Don't discriminate!"

Boycotter #5:   (Holds up placard and speaks in a chastising tone)

"FIRST-CLASS CITIZENSHIP, NOW!"

Boycotter #6: (Holds up placard and speaks in a tone as if charging people with a mission)

"AND REMEMBER ROSA PARKS!"

(The boycotters resound the words by chanting in a high tone of voice and then in a low tone: "Remember Rosa Parks" as they march around in a circle until curtains are closed)

SCENE 3: THE OLD WOMAN'S WALK

NARRATOR: Some people preferred to walk, feeling that it was a symbolic act in the struggle for justice. One driver stopped along side an elderly Black woman who was slowly making her way down the street.

Old Woman: (An old woman dressed in a hat, wearing eye-glasses, leaning on a cane, possibly, a shoulder pocket-book)

Taxi Driver: (Slows down the car and speaks in a respectful tone of voice)

"Old lady, let me give you a ride. You don't have to walk!"

Old Woman: (Looks up slowly with her hand trembling on the cane and replies—and make her point for walking).

"I'm not walking for myself, sonny. I'm walking for my children and my grandchildren!"

ACT II

MONTGOMERY IMPROVEMENT ASSOCIATION KEEPING THE BOYCOTT ALIVE

SCENE 1:   Office of the M.I.A.

(A secretary is seated at a desk with a telephone)

Rev. Abernathy: "We have received contributions from churches in practically every city in the United States."

Dr. King: "We haven't done too badly with contributions from other countries. Here's a check from Tokyo; from Singapore and from Switzerland."

NARRATOR: The Boycott was hard work: It was also expensive. It took $5,000.00 a month to run the car pool. Rich people and poor people supported the boycott in Montgomery. Then they began receiving support from all over the world.

Rev. Abernathy: "Listen to this note of encouragement"

"Your work is outstanding in the history of our country.'" (Pauses)

"Here is another interesting note:

'You have shown that decency and courage will eventually prevail.'"

Dr. King: "Here is one note I would like to believe. It says 'The entire nation salutes you.'"

NARRATOR: The work increased for the leaders, Dr. King and Rev. Abernathy, but they refused to give up. Threats were made by whites on Dr. King's life.

SCENE 2: **The Home of Dr. Martin L. King, Jr. THREATENING TELEPHONE CALL)**

(Dr. King is sleeping—telephone rings—dresses in house robe— then answers the telephone)

White Voice: "Listen nigger, we've taken all we want from you, before next week you'll be sorry you ever came to Montgomery, Alabama!"

Dr. King: (Hangs up telephone nervously.)

Mrs. King: (Mrs. King enter, dressed in house robe carrying a cup of coffee in her hand. She walks over to Dr. King and gives him a gentle pat on the back.)

"Don't worry Martin. God is with you!"

Dr. King: (Dr. King falls on bending knees in prayer. Curtains closes.)

NARRATOR: Dr. King found inner strength from prayer. When times were too hard for him, he'd steal away and pray. When it seemed as if he had been drained of courage, he was quickly revived through prayer. He could not afford to show his fear. There were too many people looking up to him for leadership.

SCENE 3: THE BOMBING OF DR. KING'S HOME

NARRATOR: The Boycott was successful, but there were still bitter days ahead. Three days later while Mrs. King and a church member, Mary Lucy, were watching television some-thing strange happened. Mrs. King's nine-week old daughter, Yoki, was asleep in the backroom of the house.

Without warning, a loud noise was heard.

(Narrator pauses for each drama-tization)

Quickly, they rushed to the back part of the house to check on the baby.

Suddenly, the bomb exploded, shattering windows and sending smoke into the room.

Mary Lucy tried to comfort Mrs. King. (Pause)

There was heavy knocking at Mrs. King's door.

Mrs. King: (Opens door.)

NARRATOR: Neighbors rushed in to help. Luckily, no one was injured.

(Pause)

NARRATOR: Later, Mrs. King's telephone rang. (Ringing of telephone)

Mrs. King: (Finds her way to the telephone and picks up the receiver)

NARRATOR: It was the voice of a woman who said:

Voice: (Behind curtain or tape.)

"Yes, I did it! I'm sorry I didn't kill all of you!"

SCENE 4: THE ANGRY MOB—NON-VIO-LENT CRUSADER

Mob Scene: (A group of Blacks talk loudly of what they are going to do to retaliate and many of them are, openly, carrying a variety of weapons.)

NARRATOR: A large number of Blacks armed themselves with guns, rocks, bats, knives, sticks and bottles.

Dr. King: (After he receives the distressful news, Dr. King returns to his home—makes his way through the crowd. He is relived when he finds that his family is safe—kisses his wife and baby).

NARRATOR: After seeing that his family was safe, Dr. King went outside to try to calm down the angry crowd.

Crowd: (Group is reluctant to put down weapons.)

Dr. King: "We are tired, tired of being segregated and humiliated! We are impatient for justice. But we will protest with love. There will be no cross burnings. No white person will be taken from his home by a hooded Negro mob and murdered. If we do this, if we protest with love, future historians will have to say, there lived a great people, a Black people who injected new meaning and dignity into the veins of civilization. I believe in nonviolence. Get rid of your weapons. We must love our white brothers no matter what they do to us. What we are doing is just, and God is with us!"

Crowd: (Tense and angry visages disappear slowly from the faces of the people—weapons are dropped two by two—the crowd begins to disperse.)

Old Man: (Walks up to Dr. King.)

             "God Bless you, Son!"

NARRATOR: On February 1, 1956, the Montgomery Improvement Association filed suit in the United States Federal District Court asking that segregation on public buses be abolished because it violated the 14th Amendment of the United States Constitution. The hearing was set for May 11, 1956.

NARRATOR: To show their anger about the political action by Blacks, the City of Montgomery began arresting some of the most respected Blacks in the City. They were accused of conspiring to destroy business in Montgomery. The first to be tried was Dr. King. He was found guilty and fined $500.00.

             Newspapers throughout the country carried these stories and put the spotlight on the *injustices* found in Montgomery, Alabama.

SCENE 5: VICTORY FOR THE MONTGOMERY IMPROVEMENT ASSOCIATION

(Stage set up at M.I.A. Office with Dr. King and Rev. Abernathy, and other workers)

NARRATOR: Finally, Dr. King and the M.I.A. received a response from the United States Federal District Court. This court found that the City's bus segregation laws of Alabama were unconstitutional. Dr. King's attorneys didn't stop there—they went on to the United States Supreme Court in Washington, D.C.

It was a long wait. By November, the spirits of Blacks were very low. For in the meantime, the City of Montgomery was still trying to destroy their boycott. But just at the right time. Dr. King and the boycotters received good news.

MONTGOMERY IMPROVEMENT ASSOCIATION OFFICE)

Reporter: (Reporter rushes in with good news.)

(Look Dr. King, here's a news release! The United States Supreme Court has ruled in your favor!"

Dr. King: (Reads the release from the newspaper)

"Alabama State and local laws requiring segregation on buses unconstitutional!"

M.I.A.: "Jubilee! Thank God! We won! We won!"

Dr. King: "Let us bow our heads to give a word of thanks."

(Curtains close)

NARRATOR: The united Blacks under the leadership of Dr. King won their fight.

(PAUSE—Curtain open)

NARRATOR: (Bus Scene)

On December 21, 1956, Dr. King got on the South Jackson Street bus. He took a seat next to the window. Reverend Glenn Smiley, a white minister, from New York got on and sat down next to Dr. King. White man and Black man, side by side, in Montgomery, Alabama went for a ride on the bus.

The Bus Boycott had lasted 381 days—until Blacks had won their rights and demands.

The Golden Literary Treasury

Martin Luther King and Rev Abernathy

In December, 1955, Mrs. Rosa Parks was told to give up her seat on a Montgomery, Alabama, bus to a white passenger, as the law required. Mrs. Parks refused. She was arrested. That arrest led to the Montgomery bus boycott.

The Day of Days, December 5

MARTIN LUTHER KING, JR.

My wife and I awoke earlier than usual on Monday morning. We were up and fully dressed by five-thirty. The day for the protest had arrived, and we were determined to see the first act of this unfolding drama. I was still saying that if we could get 60 percent cooperation the venture would be a success.

Fortunately, a bus stop was just five feet from our house. This meant that we could observe the opening stages from our front window. The first bus was to pass around six o'clock. And so we waited through an interminable half hour. I was in the kitchen drinking my coffee when I heard Coretta cry, "Martin, Martin, come quickly!" I put down my cup and ran toward the living room. As I approached the front window Coretta pointed joyfully to a slowly moving bus: "Darling, it's empty!" I could hardly believe what I saw, I knew that the South Jackson line,

Reprinted by arrangement with INTELLECTUAL PROPER-TIES MANAGEMENT, ATLANTA, GEORGIA, AS EXCLUSIVE LICENSOR OF THE KING ESTATE

which ran past our house, carried more Negro passengers than any other line in Montgomery, and that this first bus was usually filled with domestic workers going to their jobs. Would all of the other buses follow the pattern that had been set by the first? Eagerly we waited for the next bus. In fifteen minutes it rolled down the street, and, like the first, it was empty. A third bus appeared, and it too was empty of all but two white passengers.

I jumped in my car and for almost an hour I cruised down every major street and examined every passing bus. During this hour, at the peak of the morning traffic, I saw no more than eight Negro passengers riding the buses. By this time I was jubilant. Instead of the 60 percent cooperation we had hoped for, it was becoming apparent that we had reached almost 100 percent. A miracle had taken place. The once dormant and quiescent Negro community was now fully awake.

All day long it continued. At the afternoon peak the buses were still as empty of Negro passengers as they had been in the morning. Students of Alabama State College, who usually kept the South Jackson bus crowded, were cheerfully walking or thumbing rides. Job holders had either found other means of transportation or made their way on foot. While some rode in cabs or private cars, others used less conventional means. Men were seen riding mules to work, and more than one horsedrawn buggy drove the streets of Montgomery that day.

During the rush hours the sidewalks were crowded with laborers and domestic workers, many of them well past middle age, trudging patiently to their jobs and home again, sometimes as much as twelve miles. They knew why they walked, and the knowledge was evident in the way they carried themselves. And as I watched them I knew that there is nothing more majestic than the determined courage of individuals willing to suffer and sacrifice for their freedom and dignity.

Many spectators had gathered at the bus stops to watch what was happening. At first they stood quietly, but as the day progressed they began to cheer the empty buses and laugh and make jokes. Noisy youngsters could be heard singing out, "No rider today." Trailing each bus through the Negro section were two policemen on motorcycles, assigned by the city commissioners, who claimed that Negro "goon squads" had been organized to keep other Negroes from riding the buses. In the course of the day the police succeeded in making one arrest. A college student who was helping an elderly woman across the street was charged with "intimidating passengers." But the "goon squads" existed only in the commission's imagination. No one was threatened or intimidated for riding the buses; the only harassment anyone faced was that of his own conscience.

Around nine-thirty in the morning I tore myself from the action of the city streets and headed for the crowded police court. Here Mrs. Parks was being tried for disobeying the city segregation ordinance. Her attorney, Fred D. Gray—the brilliant young Negro who later became the chief counsel for the protest movement—was on hand to defend her. After the judge heard the arguments, he found Mrs. Parks guilty and fined her ten dollars and court costs (a total of fourteen dollars). She appealed the case. This was one of the first clear-cut instances in which a Negro had been convicted for disobeying the segregation law. In the past, either cases like this had been dismissed or the people involved had been charged with disorderly conduct. So in a real sense the arrest and conviction of Mrs. Parks had a two-fold impact: it was a precipitating factor to arouse the Negroes to positive action; and it was a test of the validity of the segregation law itself. I am sure that supporters of such prosecutions would have acted otherwise if they had had the prescience to look beyond the moment....

Meanwhile Roy Bennett had called several people together at three o'clock to make plans for the evening mass meeting. Everyone present was elated by the tremendous success that had already attended the protest. But beneath this feeling was the question, where do we go from here? When E. D. Nixon reported on his discussion with Abernathy and French earlier in the day, and their suggestions for an *ad hoc* organization. The group responded enthusiastically. The next job was to elect the officers for the new organization.

As soon as Bennett had opened the nominations for president, Rufus Lewis spoke from the far corner of the room: "Mr. Chairman, I would like to nominate Reverend M. L. King for president." The motion was seconded and carried, and in a matter of minutes I was unanimously elected....

With the organizational matters behind us, we turned to a discussion of the evening meeting. Several people, not wanting the reporters to know our future moves, suggested that we just sing and pray; if there were specific recommendations to be made to the people, these could be mimeographed and passed out secretly during the meeting. This, they felt, would leave the reporters in the dark. Others urged that something should be done to conceal the true identity of the leaders, feeling that if no particular name was revealed it would be safer for all involved. After a rather lengthy discussion, E. D. Nixon rose impatiently:

"We are acting like little boys," he said. "Somebody's name will have to be known, and if we are afraid we might just as well fold up right now. We must also be men enough to discuss our recommendations in the open; this idea of secretly passing something around on paper is a lot of bunk. The white folks are eventually going to find out anyway. We'd better decide now if we are going to be fearless men or scared boys."

With this forthright statement the air was cleared. Nobody would again suggest that we try to conceal our identity or avoid facing the issue head on. Nixon's courageous affirmation had given new heart to those who were about to be crippled by fear....

Immediately the resolution committee set to drafting its statement. Despite our satisfaction at the success of the protest so far, we were still concerned. Would the evening meeting be well attended? Could we hope that the fortitude and enthusiasm of the Negro community would survive more than one such day of hardship? Someone suggested that perhaps we should reconsider our decision to continue the protest. "Would it not be better," said the speaker, "to call of the protest while it is still a success rather than let it go on a few more days and fizzle out? We have already proved our united strength to the white community. If we stop now we can get anything we want from the bus company, simply because they will have the feeling that we can do it again. But if we continue, and most of the people return to the buses tomorrow or the next day, the white people will laugh at us, and we will end up getting nothing." This argument was so convincing that we almost resolved to end the protest. But we finally agreed to let the mass meeting—which was only about an hour off—be our guide. If the meeting was well attended and the people were enthusiastic, we would continue; otherwise we would call off the protest that night.

Within five blocks of the church I noticed a traffic jam. Cars were lined up as far as I could see on both sides of the street. It was a moment before it occurred to me that all of these cars were headed for the mass meeting. I had to park at least four blocks from the church, and as I started walking I noticed that hundreds of people were standing outside. In the dark night, police cars circled slowly around the area, surveying the orderly, patient, and good-humored crowd. The three or four thousand people who could not get into the church were to stand cheerfully throughout the evening listening to the proceedings on the loud-speakers that had been set up outside for their benefit. And when, near the end of the meeting, these speakers were silenced at the request of the white people in surrounding neighborhoods, the crowd would still remain quietly, content simply to be present.

It took fully fifteen minutes to push my way through to the pastor's study, where Dr. Wilson told me that the church had been packed since five o'clock. By now my doubts concerning the continued success of our venture were dispelled. The question of calling off the protest was now academic. The enthusiasm of these thousands of people swept everything along like an onrushing tidal wave.

It was some time before the remaining speakers could push their way to the rostrum through the tightly packed church. When the meeting began it was almost half an hour late. The opening hymn was the old familiar "Onward Christian Soldiers," and when that mammoth audience stood to sing, the voices outside swelling the chorus in the church, there was a mighty ring like the glad echo of heaven itself.

Rev. W. F. Alford, minister to the Beulah Baptist Church, led the congregation in prayer, followed by a reading of the Scripture by Rev. U. J. Fields, minister of the Bell Street Baptist Church. Then the chairman introduced me. As the audience applauded, I rose and stood before the pulpit. Television cameras began to shoot from all sides. The crowd grew quiet.

Without manuscript or notes, I told the story of what had happened to Mrs. Parks. Then I reviewed the long history of abuses and insults that Negro citizens had experienced on the city buses. "But there comes a time," I said, "that people get tired. We are here this evening to say to those who have mistreated us so long that we are tired—tired of being segregated and humiliated; tired of being kicked about by the brutal feet of oppression." The congregation met this statement with fervent applause. "We had no alternative but to protest." I continued. "For many years, we have shown amazing patience. We have sometimes given our white brothers the feeling that we liked the way we were being treated. But we come here tonight to be saved from that patience that makes us patient with anything less than freedom and justice." Again the audience interrupted with applause.

Briefly I justified our actions, both morally and legally. "One of the great glories of democracy is the right to protest for right." Comparing our methods with those of the White Citizens Councils and the Ku Klux Klan, I pointed out that while "these organizations are protesting for the perpetuation of injustice in the community, we are protesting for the birth of justice in the community. Their methods lead to violence and lawlessness. But in our protest there will be no cross burnings. No white person will be taken from his home by a hooded Negro mob and brutally murdered. There will be no threats and intimidation. We will be guided by the highest principles of law and order."

With this groundwork for militant action, I moved on to words of caution. I urged the people not to force anybody to refrain from riding the buses. "Our method will be that of persuasion, not coercion. We will only say to the people, 'Let your conscience be your guide.'" Emphasizing the Christian doctrine of love, "our actions must be guided by the deepest principles of our Christian faith. Love must be our regulating ideal. Once again we must hear the words of Jesus echoing across the centuries: 'Love your enemies, bless them that curse you, and pray for them that despitefully use you.' If we fail to do this our protest will end up as a meaningless drama on the stage of history, and its memory will be shrouded with ugly garments of shame. In spite of the mistreatment that we have confronted we must not become bitter, and end up by hating our white brothers.

As Booker T. Washington said, 'Let no man pull you so low as to make you hate him,'" Once more the audience responded enthusiastically.

Then came my closing statement. "If you will protest courageously, and yet with dignity and Christian love, when the history books are written in future generations, the historians will have to pause and say, 'There lived a great people—a black people—who injected new meaning and dignity into the veins of civilization.' This is our challenge and our overwhelming responsibility." As I took my seat the people rose to their feet and applauded. I was thankful to God that the message had gotten over and that the task of combining the militant and the moderate had been at least partially accomplished. The people had been as enthusiastic when I urged them to love as they were when I urged them to protest.

As I sat listening to the continued applause I realized that this speech had evoked more response than any speech or sermon I had ever delivered, and yet it was virtually unprepared. I came to see for the first time what the older preachers meant when they said, "Open your mouth and God will speak for you." While I would not let this experience tempt me to overlook the need for continued preparation, it would always remind me that God can transform man's weakness into his glorious opportunity.

When Mrs. Parks was introduced from the rostrum by E. N. French, the audience responded by giving her a standing ovation. She was their heroine. They saw in her courageous person the symbol of their hopes and aspirations.

Now the time had come for the all-important resolution. Ralph Abernathy read the words slowly and forcefully. The main substance of the resolution called upon the Negroes not to resume riding the buses until (1) courteous treatment by the bus operators was guaranteed: (2) passengers were seated on a first-come, first-served basis—Negroes seated from the back of the bus toward the front while whites seated from the front toward the back; (3) Negro bus operators were employed on predominantly Negro routes. At the words "All in favor of the motion stand," every person to a man stood up, and those who were already standing raised their hands. Cheers began to ring out from both inside and outside. The motion was carried unanimously. The people had expressed their determination not to ride the buses until conditions were changed.

At this point I had to leave the meeting and rush to the other side of town to speak at a YMCA banquet. As I drove away my heart was full. I had never seen such enthusiasm for freedom. And yet this enthusiasm was tempered by amazing self-discipline. The unity of purpose and *esprit de corps* of these people had been indescribably moving. No historian would ever be able to interpret it adequately. One had to be a part of the experience really to understand it.

At the Ben Moore Hotel, as the elevator slowly moved up to the roof garden where the banquet was being held, I said to myself, victory is already won, no matter how long we struggle to attain the three points of the resolution. It is a victory infinitely larger than the bus situation. The real victory was in the mass meeting, where thousands of black people stood revealed with a new sense of dignity and destiny....

That night we were starting a movement that would gain national recognition; whose echoes would ring in the ears of people of every nation; a movement that would astound the oppressor, and bring new hope to the oppressed. That night was Montgomery's moment in history.

Martin Luther King sitting in the Birmington Jail.

April 16, 1963
Birmingham, Alabama

Letter from Birmingham Jail

My dear fellow clergymen:
While confined here in the Birmingham city jail, I came across your recent statement calling my present activities "unwise and untimely." Seldom do I pause to answer criticism of my work and ideas.... But since I feel that you are men of genuine good will and that your criticisms are sincerely set forth, I want to try to answer your statement in what I hope will be patient and reasonable terms....

I think I should indicate why I am here in Birmingham, since you have been influenced by the view which argues against "outsiders coming in."... I am here because I have organizational ties here.... But more basically, I am in Birmingham because injustice is here....

Moreover, I am cognizant of the interrelatedness of all communities and states. I cannot sit idly by in Atlanta and not be concerned about what happens in Birmingham. Injustice anywhere is a threat to justice everywhere. We are caught in an inescapable network of mutuality, tied in a single garment of destiny.

Whatever affects one directly, affects all indirectly. Never again can we afford to live with the narrow, provincial "outside agitator" idea. Anyone who lives inside the United States can never be considered an outsider anywhere within its bounds.

You deplore the demonstrations taking place in Birmingham. But your statement, I am sorry to say, fails to express a similar concern for the conditions that brought about the demonstrations.

I am sure that none of you would want to rest content with the superficial kind of social analysis that deals merely with effects and does not grapple with underlying causes. It is unfortunate that demonstrations are taking place in Birmingham, but it is even more unfortunate that the city's white power structure left the Negro community with no alternative.

In any nonviolent campaign there are four basic steps: collection of the facts to determine whether injustices exist; negotiation; self-purification; and direct action. We have gone through all these steps in Birmingham.

There can be no gainsaying the fact that racial injustice engulfs this community. Birmingham is probably the most thoroughly segregated city in the United States. Its ugly record of brutality is widely known. Negroes have experienced grossly unjust treatment in the courts. There have been more unresolved bombings of Negro homes and churches in Birmingham than in any other city in the nation. These are the hard, brutal facts of the case....

On the basis of these conditions, Negro leaders sought to negotiate fathers. But the latter consistently refused to engage in good-faith negotiation. Then, last September, came the opportunity to talk with leaders of Birmingham's economic community. In the course of negotiations, certain promises were made by the merchants—for example, to remove the stores humiliating racial signs.

On the basis of these promises, the Reverend Fred Shuttlesworth and the leaders of the Alabama Christian Movement for Human Rights agreed to a moratorium on all demonstrations. As the weeks and months went by, we realized that we were the victims of a broken promise. A few signs, briefly removed, returned; the others remained.

As in so many past experiences, our hopes had been blasted, and the shadow of deep disappointment settled upon us. We had no alternative except to prepare for direct action, whereby we would present our very bodies as a means of laying our case before the conscience of the local and the national community.

Mindful of the difficulties involved, we decided to undertake the process of self-purification. We began a series of workshops on nonviolence, and we repeatedly asked ourselves: "Are you able to accept blows without retaliation?" "Are you able to endure the ordeal of jail?"...

You may well ask, "Why direct action?" Why sit-ins, marches and so forth? Isn't negotiation a better path?" You are quite right in calling for negotiation. Indeed, this is the very purpose of direct action. Non-violent direct action seeks to create such a crisis and foster such a tension that a community which has constantly refused to negotiate is forced to confront the issue. It seeks so to dramatize the issue that it can no longer be ignored.

My citing the creating of tension as part of the work of the nonviolent resister may sound rather shocking. But I must confess that I am not afraid of the word "tension." I have earnestly opposed violent tension, but there is a type of constructive, nonviolent tension which is necessary for growth.

Just as Socrates felt that it was necessary to create a tension in the mind so that individuals could rise from the bondage of myths and half-truths to the unfettered realm of creative analysis and objective appraisal, so must we see the need for nonviolent gadflies to create the kind of tension in society that will help men rise from the dark depths of prejudice and racism to the majestic heights of understanding and brotherhood.

The purpose of our direct-action program is to create a situation so crisis-packed that it will in-evitably open the door to negotiation. I therefore con-cur with you in your call for negotiation. Too long has our beloved Southland been bogged down in a tragic effort to live in monologue rather than dialogue.

One of the basic points in your statement is that the action that I and my associates have taken in Birmingham is untimely. Some have asked: "Why didn't you give the new city administration time to act?" The only answer that I can give to this query is that the new Birmingham administration must be prodded about as much as the outgoing one, before it will act....

We have not made a single gain in civil rights without determined legal and nonviolent pressure.... Lamentably, it is an historical fact that privileged groups seldom give up their privileges voluntarily. Individuals may see the moral light and voluntarily give up their unjust posture; but, as Reinhold Niebuhr has reminded us, groups tend to be more immoral than individuals.

We know through painful experience that freedom is never voluntarily given by the oppressor. It must be demanded by the oppressed. Frankly, I have yet to engage in a direct-action campaign that was "well timed" in view of those who have not suffered unduly from the disease of segregation.

For years now I have heard the word "Wait!" It rings in the ear of every Negro with piercing familiarity. This "Wait!" has almost always meant "Never." We must come to see, with one of our distinguished jurists, that "justice too long delayed is justice denied."

We have waited for more than 340 years for our constitutional and God-given rights. The nations of Asia and Africa are moving with jetlike speed toward gaining political independence, but we still creep at horse-and-buggy pace toward gaining a cup of coffee at a lunch counter. Perhaps it is easy for those who have never felt the stinging darts of segregation to say, "Wait."

But when you have seen vicious mobs lynch your mothers and fathers at will and drown your sisters and brothers at whim;

when you have seen hate-filled policemen curse, kick and even kill your black brothers and sisters;

when you see the vast majority of your twenty million Negro brothers smothering in an airtight cage of poverty in the midst of an affluent society;

when you suddenly find your tongue twisted and your speech stammering as you seek to explain to your six-year-old daughter why she can't go to the public amusement park that has just been advertised on television, and see tears welling up in her eyes when she is told that Funtown is closed to colored children, and see ominous clouds of inferiority beginning to form in her little mental sky, and see her beginning to distort her personality by developing an unconscious bitterness toward white people;

when you have to concoct an answer for a five-year-old son who is asking, "Daddy, why do white people treat colored people so mean?";

when you take a cross-country drive and find it necessary to sleep night after night in the uncomfortable corners of your automobile because no motel will accept you;

when you are humiliated day in and day out by nagging signs reading "white" and "colored";

when your first name becomes "nigger," your middle name becomes "boy" (however old you are) and your last name becomes "John," and your wife and mother are never given the respected title "Mrs.";

when you are harried by day and haunted by night by the fact that you are a Negro, living constantly at tiptoe stance, never quite knowing what to expect next, and are plagued with inner fears and outer resentments;

when you are forever fighting a degenerating sense of "nobodiness"—then you will understand why we find it difficult to wait.

There comes a time when the cup of endurance runs over, and men are no longer willing to be plunged into the abyss of despair. I hope, sirs, you can understand our legitimate and unavoidable impatience.

You express a great deal of anxiety over our willingness to break laws. This is certainly a legitimate concern. Since we so diligently urge people to obey the Supreme Court's decision of 1954 outlawing segregation in the public schools, at first glance it may seem rather paradoxical for us consciously to break laws.

One may well ask: "How can you advocate breaking some laws and obeying others?" The answer lies in the fact that there are two types of laws: just and unjust. I would be the first to advocate obeying just laws. One has not only a legal but a moral responsibility to obey just laws. Conversely, one has a moral responsibility to disobey unjust laws. I would agree with St. Augustine that "an unjust law is no law at all."

Now, what is the difference between the two? How does one determine whether a law is just or unjust? A just law is a man-made code that squares with the moral law or the law of God. An unjust law is a code that is out of harmony with the moral law.

To put it in the terms of St. Thomas Aquinas: An unjust law is a human law that is not rooted in eternal law and natural law. Any law that uplifts human personality is just. Any law that degrades human personality is unjust.

All segregation statutes are unjust because segregation distorts the soul and damages the personality. It gives the segregator a false sense of superiority and the segregated a false sense of inferiority....

Let us consider a more concrete example of just and unjust laws. An unjust law is a code that a numerical or power majority group compels a minority group to obey but does not make binding on itself. This is *difference* made legal. By the same token, a just law is a code that a majority compels a minority to follow and that it is willing to follow itself. This is *sameness* made legal.

Let me give another explanation. A law is unjust if it is inflicted on a minority that, as a result of being denied the right to vote, had no part in enacting or devising the law. Who can say that the legislature of Alabama which set up the state's segregation laws was democratically elected?

Throughout Alabama all sorts of devious methods are used to prevent Negroes from becoming registered voters, and there are some counties in which, even though Negroes constitute a majority of the population, not a single Negro is registered. Can any law enacted under such circumstances be considered democratically structured?

Sometimes a law is just on its face and unjust in its application. For instance, I have been arrested on a charge of parading without a permit. Now, there is nothing wrong in having an ordinance which requires a permit for a parade. But such an ordinate becomes unjust when it is used to maintain segregation and to deny citizens the First-Amendment privilege of peaceful assembly and protest.

I hope you are able to see the distinction I am trying to point out. In no sense do I advocate evading or defying the law, as would the rabid segregationist. That would lead to anarchy.

One who breaks an unjust law must do so openly, lovingly and with a willingness to accept the penalty. I submit that an individual who breaks a law that conscience tells him is unjust, and who willingly accepts the penalty of imprisonment in order to arouse the conscience of the community over its injustice, is in reality expressing the highest respect for law.

Of course, there is nothing new about this kind of civil disobedience. It was evidenced sublimely in the refusal of Shadrach, Meshach, and Abednego to obey the laws of Nebuchadnezzar, on the ground that a higher moral law was at stake. It was practiced superbly by the early Christians, who were willing to face hungry lions and the excruciating pain of chopping blocks rather than submit to certain unjust laws of the Roman Empire.

To a degree, academic freedom is a reality today because Socrates practiced civil disobedience. In our own nation, the Boston Tea Party represented a massive act of civil disobedience.

We should never forget that everything Adolf Hitler did in Germany was "legal" and everything the Hungarian freedom fighters did in Hungary was "illegal." It was "illegal" to aid and comfort a Jew in Hitler's Germany. Even so, I am sure that, had I lived in Germany at the time, I would have aided and comforted my Jewish brothers. If today I lived in a Communist country where certain principles dear to the Christian faith are suppressed, I would openly advocate disobeying that country's anti-religious laws.

I must make two honest confessions to you, my Christian and Jewish brothers. First, I must confess that over the past few years I have been gravely disappointed with the white moderate. I have almost reached the regrettable conclusion that the Negro's great stumbling block in his stride toward freedom is not the White Citizen's Counciler or the Ku Klux Klanner, but the white moderate, who is more devoted to "order" than to justice; who prefers a negative peace which is the absence of tension to a positive peace which is the presence of justice; who constantly says, "I agree with you in the goal you seek, but I cannot agree with your methods of direct action"; who paternalistically believes he can set the timetable for another man's freedom; who lives by a mythical concept of time and who constantly advises the Negro to wait for a "more convenient season."

Shallow understanding from people of good will is more frustrating that absolute misunderstanding from people of ill will. Lukewarm acceptance is much more bewildering than outright rejection.

I had hoped that the white moderate would understand that law and order exist for the purpose of establishing justice and that when they fail in this purpose they become the dangerously structured dams that block the flow of social progress.

I had hoped that the white moderate would understand that the present tension in the South is a necessary phase of the transition from an obnoxious negative peace, in which the Negro passively accepted his unjust plight, to a substantive and positive peace, in which all men will respect the dignity and worth of human personality.

Actually, we who engage in non-violent direct action are not the creators of tension. We merely bring to the surface the hidden tension that is already alive. We bring it out in the open, where it can be seen and dealt with. Like a boil that can never be cured so long as it is covered up but must be opened with all its ugliness to the natural medicines of air and light, injustice must be exposed, with all the tension its exposure creates, to the light of human conscience and the air of national opinion, before it can be cured.

In your statement you assert that our actions, even though peaceful, must be condemned because they precipitate violence. But is this a logical assertion? Isn't this like condemning a robbed man because his possession of money precipitated the evil act of robbery?....

We must come to see that, as the federal courts have consistently affirmed, it is wrong to urge an individual to cease his efforts to gain his basic constitutional rights because the quest may precipitate violence. Society must protect the robbed and punish the robber.

I had also hoped that the white moderate would reject the myth concerning time in relation to the struggle for freedom.... Actually, time itself is neutral; it can be used either destructively or constructively. More and more I feel that the people of ill will have used time much more effectively than have the people of good will. We will have to repent in this generation not merely for the hateful words and actions of the bad people, but for the appalling silence of the good people.

Human progress never rolls in on wheels of inevitability, it comes through the tireless efforts of men willing to be co-workers with God, and without this hard work, time itself becomes an ally of the forces of stagnation. We must use time creatively, in the knowledge that the time is always ripe to do right.

Now is the time to make real the promise of democracy and transform our pending national elegy into a creative psalm of brotherhood. Now is the time to lift our national policy from the quicksand of racial injustice to the solid rock of human dignity.

You speak of our activity in Birmingham as extreme. At first I was rather disappointed that fellow clergymen would see my nonviolent effort as those of an extremist. I began thinking about the fact that I stand in the middle of two opposing forces in the Negro community.

One is the force of complacency, made up in part of Negroes who, as a result of long years of oppression, are so drained of self-respect and a sense of "somebodiness" that they have adjusted to segregation; and in part of a few middle-class Negroes who, because of a degree of academic or economic security and because in some ways they profit by segregation, have become insensitive to the problems of the masses.

The other force is one of bitterness and hatred, and it comes perilously close to advocating violence. It is expressed in the various black nationalist groups that are springing up across the nation, the largest and best-known being Elijah Muhammad's Muslim movement. Nourished by the Negro's frustration over the continued existence of racial discrimination, this movement is made up of people who have lost faith in America, who have absolutely repudiated Christianity, and who have concluded that the white man is an incorrigible "devil."

I have tried to stand between these two forces, saying that we need emulate neither the "do-nothingism" of the complacent nor the hatred and despair of the black nationalist. For there is the more excellent way of love and nonviolent protest. I am grateful to God that, through the influence of the Negro church, the way of nonviolence became an integral part of our struggle.

If this philosophy had not emerged, by now many streets of the South would, I am convinced, be flowing with blood. And I am further convinced that if our white brothers dismiss as "rabble-rousers" and "outside agitators" those of us who employ nonviolent direct action, and if they refuse to support our nonviolent efforts, millions of Negroes will, out of frustration and despair, seek solace and security in black-nationalist ideologies—a development that would inevitably lead to a frightening racial nightmare.

Oppressed people cannot remain oppressed forever. The yearning for freedom eventually manifests itself, and that is what has happened to the American Negro. Something within has reminded him of his birthright of freedom, and something without has reminded him that it can be gained. Consciously or unconsciously, he has been caught up by the Zeitgeist, and with his black brothers of Africa and his brown and yellow brothers of Asia, South America and the Caribbean, the United States Negro is moving with a sense of great urgency toward the promised land of racial justice.

If one recognizes this vital urge that has engulfed the Negro community, one should readily understand why public demonstrations are taking place. The Negro has many pent-up resentments and latent frustrations, and he must release them. So let him march; let him make prayer pilgrimages to the city hall; let him go on freedom rides—and try to understand why he must do so.

If his repressed emotions are not released in nonviolent ways, they will seek expression through violence; this is not a threat but a fact of history. So I have not said to my people, "Get rid of your discontent." Rather, I have tried to say that this normal and healthy discontent can be channeled into the creative outlet of nonviolent direct action. And now this approach is being termed extremist.

But though I was initially disappointed at being categorized as an extremist, as I continued to think about the matter I gradually gained a measure of satisfaction from the label.

Was not Jesus an extremist for love: "Love your enemies, bless them that curse you, do good to them that hate you, and pray for them which despitefully use you, and persecute you."

Was not Amos an extremist for justice: "Let justice roll down like waters and righteousness like an everflowing stream."...

And John Bunyan: "I will stay in jail to the end of my days before I make a butchery of my conscience."

And Abraham Lincoln: "This nation cannot survive half slave and half free." And Thomas Jefferson: "We hold these truths to be self-evident, that all men are created equal...."

So the question is not whether we will be extremists, but what kind of extremists will we be. Will we be extremists for hate or for love? Will we be extremists for the preservation of injustice or for the extension of justice?... Perhaps the South, the nation, and the world are in dire need of creative extremists.

I had hoped that the white moderate would see this need. Perhaps I was too optimistic; perhaps I should have realized that few members of the oppressor race can understand the deep groans and passionate yearnings of the oppressed race, and still fewer have the vision to see that injustice must be rooted out by strong, persistent, and determined action.

I am thankful, however, that some of out white brothers in the South have grasped the meaning of this social revolution and committed themselves to it. They are still all too few in quantity, but they are big in quality. Some—such as Ralph McGill, Lillian Smith, Harry Golden, James McBride Dabbs, Ann Braden, and Sarah Patton Boyle—have written about our struggle in eloquent and prophetic terms.

Others have marched with us down nameless streets of the South. They have languished in filthy, roach-infested jails, suffering the abuse and brutality of policemen who view them as "dirty nigger-lovers." Unlike so many of their moderate brothers and sisters, they have recognized the urgency of the moment and sensed the need for powerful "action" antidotes to combat the disease of segregation.

Let me take note of my other major disappointment with the white church and its leadership.

Of course, there are some notable exceptions. I am not unmindful of the fact that each of you has taken some significant stands on this issue. I commend you, Reverend Stallings, for your Christian stand on this past Sunday, in welcoming Negroes to your worship service on a nonsegregated basis. I commend the Catholic leaders of this state for integrating Spring Hill College several years ago.

But despite these notable exceptions, I must honestly reiterate that I have been disappointed with the church. I do not say this as one of those negative critics who can always find something wrong with the church. I say this as a minister of the gospel, who loves the church; who has nurtured in its bosom;

who has been sustained by its spiritual blessings and who will remain true to it as long as the cord of life shall lengthen.

When I was suddenly catapulted into the leadership of the bus protest in Montgomery, Alabama, a few years ago, I felt we would be supported by the white church. I felt that the white ministers, priests and rabbis of the South would be among our strongest allies. Instead, some have been out right opponents, refusing to understand the freedom movement and misrepresenting its leaders; all too many others have been more cautious than courageous and have remained silent behind the anesthetizing security of stained-glass windows.

In spite of my shattered dreams, I came to Birmingham with the hope that the white religious leadership of this community would see the justice of our cause and, with deep moral concern, would serve as the channel through which our just grievances could reach the power structure. I had hoped that each of you would understand. But again I have been disappointed.

I have heard numerous southern religious leaders admonish their worshipers to comply with a desegregation decision because it is the law, but I have longed to hear white ministers declare: "Follow this decree because integration is morally right and because the Negro is your brother."

In the midst of blatant injustices inflicted upon the Negro, I have watched white churchmen stand on the sideline and mouth pious irrelevancies and sanctimonious trivialities. In the midst of a mighty struggle to rid our nation of racial and economic injustice, I have heard many ministers say: "Those are social issues, with which the gospel has no real concern." And I have watched many churches commit themselves to a completely otherworldly religion which makes a strange, un-Biblical distinction between body and soul; between the sacred and the secular....

I hope the church as a whole will meet the challenge of this decisive hour. But even if the church does not come to the aid of justice, I have no despair about the future. I have no fear about the outcome of our struggle in Birmingham, even if our motives are at present misunderstood. We will reach the goal of freedom in Birmingham and all over the nation, because the goal of America is freedom.

Abused and scorned though we may be, our destiny is tied up with America's destiny. Before the pilgrims landed at Plymouth, we were here. For more than two centuries our forebears labored in this country, without wages; they made cotton king; they built the homes of their masters while suffering gross injustice and shameful humiliation—and yet out of a bottomless vitality they continued to thrive and develop.

If the inexpressible cruelties of slavery could not stop us, the opposition we now face will surely fail. We will win our freedom because the sacred heritage of our nation and the eternal will of God are embodied in our echoing demands.

Before closing I feel impelled to mention one other point in your statement that has troubled me profoundly. You warmly commended the Birmingham police force for keeping "order" and "preventing violence."

I doubt that you would have so warmly commended the police force if you had seen its dogs sinking their teeth into unarmed, nonviolent Negroes. I doubt that you would so quickly commend the policemen if you were to observe their ugly and inhumane treatment of Negroes here in the city jail; if you were to watch them push and curse old Negro women and young Negro girls; if you were to see them slap and kick old Negro men and young Negro boys; if you were to observe them, as they did on two occasions, refuse to give us food because we wanted to sing our grace together. I cannot join you in your praise of the Birmingham police department.

It is true that the police have exercised a degree of discipline in handling the demonstrators. In this sense they have conducted themselves rather "nonviolently" in public. But for what purpose? To preserve the evil system of segregation.

Over the past few years I have consistently preached that nonviolence demands that the means we use must be as pure as the ends we seek. I have tried to make clear that it is wrong to use immoral means to attain moral ends. But now I must affirm that it is just as wrong, or perhaps even more so, to use moral means to preserve immoral ends.... As T. S. Eliot has said, "The last temptation is the greatest treason; To do the right deed for the wrong reason."

I wish you had commended the Negro sit-inners and demonstrators of Birmingham for their sublime courage, their willingness to suffer, and their amazing discipline in the midst of great provocation. One day the South will recognize its real heroes. They will be the James Merediths, with the noble sense of purpose that enables them to face jeering and hostile mobs, and with the agonizing loneliness that characterizes the life of the pioneer. They will be old, oppressed, battered Negro women, symbolized in a seventy-two-year-old woman in Montgomery, Alabama, who rose up with a sense of dignity and with her people decided not to ride segregated buses, and who responded with ungrammatical profundity to one who inquired about her weariness: "My feets is tired, but my soul is at rest."

They will be the young high school and college students, the young ministers of the gospel and a host of their elders, courageously and nonviolently sitting in at lunch counters and willingly going to jail for conscience' sake. One day the South will know that when these disinherited children of God sat down at lunch counters, they were in reality standing up for what is best in the American dream and for the most sacred values in our Judaeo-Christian heritage, thereby bringing our nation back to those wells of democracy which were dug deep by the founding fathers in their formulation of the Constitution and the Declaration of Independence.

Never before have I written so long a letter. I'm afraid it is much too long to take your precious time. I can assure you that it would have been much shorter if I had been writing from a comfortable desk, but what else can one do when he is alone in a narrow jail cell, other than write long letters, think long thoughts and pray long prayers?...

Yours for the cause of peace and brotherhood,

Martin Luther King, Jr.

Martin Luther King addressing March on Washington Crowd

"I HAVE A DREAM": DR. KING'S SPEECH

I am happy to join with you today in what will go down in history as the greatest demonstration for freedom in the history of our nation.

Five score years ago, a great American, in whose symbolic shadow we stand today, signed the Emancipation Proclamation. This momentous decree is a great beacon light of hope to millions of Negro slaves who had been seared in the flames of withering injustice. It came as a joyous daybreak to end the long night of their captivity.

But 100 years later, the Negro still is not free. One hundred years later, the life of the Negro is still badly crippled by the manacles of segregation and the chains of discrimination. One hundred years later, the Negro lives on a lonely island of poverty in the midst of a vast ocean of material prosperity. One hundred years later, the Negro is still languished in the corners of American society and finds himself in exile in his own land. So we've come here today to dramatize a shameful condition.

In a sense, we've come to our nation's capital to cash a check. When the architects of our republic wrote the magnificent words of the Constitution and the Declaration of Independence, they were signing a promissory note to which every American was to fall heir. This note was a promise that all men—yes, black men as well as white men—would be guaranteed the unalienable rights of life, liberty and the pursuit of happiness.

It is obvious today that America has defaulted on this promissory note insofar as her citizens of color are concerned. Instead of honoring this sacred obligation, America has given the Negro people a bad check, a check which has come back marked "insufficient funds."

But we refuse to believe that the bank of justice is bankrupt. We refuse to believe that there are insufficient funds in the great vaults of opportunity of this nation. So we've come to cash this check, a check that will give us upon demand the riches of freedom and the security of justice.

We have also come to this hallowed spot to remind America of the fierce urgency of now. This is no time to engage in the luxury of cooling off or to take the tranquilizing drug of gradualism. Now is the time to make real the promises of democracy. Now is the time to rise from the dark and desolate valley of segregation to the sunlit path of racial justice. Now is the time to lift brotherhood. Now is the time to make justice a reality for all of God's children.

It would be fatal for the nation to overlook the urgency of the moment. This sweltering summer of the Negro's legitimate discontent will not pass until there is an invigorating autumn of freedom and equality—1963 is not an end, but a beginning. Those who hope that the Negro needed to blow off steam and will now be content will have a rude awakening if the nation returns to business as usual.

There will be neither rest nor tranquility in America until the Negro is granted his citizenship rights. The whirlwinds of revolt will continue to shake the foundations of our nation until the bright day of justice emerges.

And that is something that I must say to my people who stand on the worn threshold which leads into the palace of justice. In the process of gaining our rightful place we must not be guilty of wrongful deeds. Let us not seek to satisfy our thirst for freedom by drinking from the cup of bitterness and hatred.

We must forever conduce our struggle on the high plane of dignity and discipline. We must not allow our creative protests to degenerate into physical violence. Again and again we must rise to the majestic heights of meeting physical force with soul force. The marvelous new militancy which has engulfed the Negro community must not lead to distrust all white people, for many of our white brothers, as evidenced by their presence here today, have come to realize that their destiny is tied up with our destiny. They have come to realize that their freedom is inextricably bound to our freedom. We cannot walk alone. And as we walk, we must make the pledge that we shall always march ahead. We cannot turn back.

There are those who are asking the devotees of civil rights, "When will you be satisfied?" We can never be satisfied as long as our bodies, heavy with the fatigue of travel, cannot gain lodging in the motels of the highways and the hotels of the cities.

We cannot be satisfied as long as the Negro's basic mobility is from a smaller ghetto to a larger one.

We can never be satisfied as long as children are stripped of their adulthood and robbed of their dignity of signs stating, "For Whites Only."

We cannot be satisfied as long as the Negro in Mississippi cannot vote and the Negro in New York believes he has nothing for which to vote.

No, no, we are not satisfied and we will not be satisfied until justice rolls down like waters and righteousness like a mighty stream.

I am not unmindful that some of you have come out of great trials and tribulation. Some of you have come fresh from narrow jail cells. Some of you have come from areas where your quest for freedom left you battered by the storms of persecution and staggering by the winds of police brutality. You have been the veterans of creative suffering. Continue to work with the faith that unearned suffering is redemptive.

Go back to Mississippi, go back to Alabama, go back to South Carolina, go back to Georgia, go back to Louisiana, go back to the slums and ghettos of our Northern cities, knowing that somehow this situation can and will be changed. Let us not wallow in the valley of despair.

I say to you today, my friends, though, even though we face the difficulties of today and tomorrow, I still have a dream. It is a dream deeply rooted in the American dream. I have a dream that one day this nation will rise up and live out the true meaning of its creed: "We hold these Truths to be self-evident, that all Men are created equal."

I have a dream that one day on the red hills of Georgia sons of former slaves and sons of former slave-owners will be able to sit down together at the table of brotherhood. I have a dream that one day even the state of Mississippi, a state sweltering with the heat of injustice, sweltering with the heat of oppression, will be transformed into an oasis of freedom and justice.

I have a dream that my four little children will one day live in a nation where they will not be judged by the color of their skin but by the content of their character. I have a dream...

I have a dream that one day in Alabama, with its vicious racists, with its governor having his lips dripping with the words of interposition and nullification, one day right there in Alabama, little black boys and little black girls will be able to join hands with little white boys and little white girls as sisters and brothers. I have a dream today...

I have a dream that one day every valley shall be exalted, every hill and mountain shall be made low. The rough places will be made plain, and the crooked places will be made straight. And the glory of the Lord shall be revealed, and all flesh shall see it together. This is our hope. This is the faith that I go back to the South with.

With this faith we will be able to hew out of the mountain of despair a stone of hope. With this faith we will be able to transform the jangling discords of our nation into a beautiful symphony of brotherhood. With this faith we will be able to work together, to pray together, to struggle together, to go to jail together, to stand up for freedom together, knowing that we will be free one day.

This will be the day when all of God's children will be able to sing with new meaning, "My country, 'tis of thee, sweet land of liberty, of thee I sing. Land where my fathers died, land of the Pilgrim's pride, from every mountainside, let freedom ring." And if America is to be a great nation, this must become true.

So let freedom ring from the prodigious hilltops of New Hampshire. Let freedom ring from the mighty mountains of New York. Let freedom ring from the heightening Alleghenies of Pennsylvania. Let freedom ring from the snow-capped Rockies of Colorado. Let freedom ring from the curvaceous slopes of California.

But not only that. Let freedom ring from Stone Mountain of Georgia. Let freedom ring from Lookout Mountain of Tennessee. Let freedom ring from every hill and molehill of Mississippi, from every mountainside. Let freedom ring...

When we allow freedom to ring—when we let it ring from every village and every hamlet, from every state and every city, we will be able to speed up that day when all of God's children, black men and white men, Jews and gentiles, Protestants and Catholics, will be able to join hands and sing, in the words of the old Negro spiritual, "Free at last, free at last, thank God almighty, we are free at last."

The Purpose of Education

January-February 1947
Atlanta, GA

As I engage in the so-called "bull sessions" around and about the school I too often find that most college men have a misconception of the purpose of education. Most of the "brethren" think that education should equip them with the proper instruments of exploitation so that they can forever trample over the masses. Still others think that education should furnish them with noble ends rather than means to an end.

It seems to me that education has a two-fold function to perform in the life of man and in society: the one is utility and the other is culture. Education must enable a man to become more efficient, to achieve with increasing facility the legitimate goals of his life.

Education must also train one for quick, resolute and effective thinking. To think incisively and to think for one's self is very difficult. We are prone to let our mental life become invaded by legions of half truths, prejudices, and propaganda. At this point, I often wonder whether or not education is fulfilling its purpose. A great majority of the so-called educated people do not think logically and scientifically. Even the press, the classroom, the platform, and the pulpit in many instances do not give us objective and unbiased truths. To save man from the morass of propaganda, in my opinion, is one of the chief aims of education. Education must enable one to sift and weigh evidence, to discern the true from the false, the real from the unreal, and the facts from the fiction.

The function of education, therefore, is to teach one to think intensively and to think critically. But education which stops with efficiency may prove the greatest menace to society. The most dangerous criminal may be the gifted with reason, but with no morals.

The late Eugene Talmadge, in my opinion, possessed one of the better minds of Georgia, or even America. Moreover, he wrote the Phi Beta Kappa key. By all measuring rods, Mr. Talmadge could think critically and intensively; yet he contends that I am an inferior being. Are those the types of men we call educated?

We must remember that intelligence is not enough. Intelligence plus character—that is the goal of true education. The complete education gives one not only power of concentration, but worthy objectives upon which to concentrate. The broad education will, therefore, transmit to one not only the accumulated knowledge of the race but also the accumulated experience of social living.

If we are not careful, our colleges will produce a group of closed-minded, unscientific, illogical propagandists, consumed with immoral acts. Be careful, "brethren!" Be careful, teachers!

Dr. Martin Luther King, Jr.
Maroon Tiger (January-February 1947): 10.

The Purpose of Education

Dr. Martin L. King, Jr.   January-February 1947
Maroon Tiger:10   Atlanta, GA

A CRITICAL ANALYSIS:
Exploring the Meaning

I. What concern was Martin L. King addressing in
the first paragraph of, The Purpose of Education:

As I engage in the so-called "bull sessions"
around and about the school I too often find

Dr. King being congratulated after being pre-
sented with the Nobel Peace prize

that most college men have a misconception of the purpose of education. Most of the "brethren" think that education should equip them with the proper instruments of exploitation so that they can forever trample over the masses. Still others think that education should furnish them with noble ends rather than means to an end.

II. What is the two-fold function of education as discussed by Martin L. King and what concepts are used to support his frame of thought?

III. What warning is Martin L. King presenting about the danger of isolating intelligence from character in education? Critique the passage below to provide a response:

We must remember that intelligence is not enough. Intelligence plus character-that is the goal of true education. The complete education gives one not only power of concentration, but worthy objectives upon which to concentrate. The broad education will, therefore, transmit to one not only the accumulated knowledge of the race but also the accumulated experience of social living.

If we are not careful, our colleges will produce a group of close-minded, unscientific, illogical propagandists, consumed with immoral acts. Be careful, "brethren!" Be careful teachers!

The legacy of Martin Luther King, Jr.

by Coretta Scott King

We have set in motion a great celebration of freedom and justice, in honor of America's hero and patriot, Martin Luther King, Jr.

When Martin began his career, the principles of social justice for which he stood were very controversial. But by the end of his career he was a widely respected leader of international stature, who helped lead an extraordinary revolution in America's laws and customs. Martin's moving example of dignity in the face of threats and hatred gave the whole nation a new hero to admire and emulate.

Martin knew that America's democracy was not perfect. But he also knew that, when aroused, America's conscience could be a powerful force for reform. His unique combination of moral leadership and practical political wisdom enlisted America's conscience on the side of peaceful change.

His memory is engraved in the hearts and minds of his fellow Americans, and it is appropriate, as the

Coretta S. King

President and the Congress have said, to remember and honor the values for which he stood. Each year, Martin's national birthday celebration will rekindle in the hearts of all our people a new pride in America, a determination to make it an even greater nation.

It will also spark a new appreciation for its son, who was born into a world where bigotry and racism still hold sway. But before he died, he contributed immeasurably to the human rights of all people.

In my travels to the 50 states and U.S. territories as chairperson of the King Federal Holiday Commission, I find that Americans from all walks of life and every political persuasion share a common enthusiasm and excitement as we prepare to celebrate what President Reagan has called "A Celebration of Freedom and Justice to Unite All Our Citizens."

There is a spirit of unity and good will sweeping this land. People of all races, religions, classes, politics and stations in life are coming together and putting aside differences in a spirit of reconciliation to make Monday, January 20, 1986 "Martin's Day," a day of great national unity and renewed patriotism consistent with the nonviolent tradition of the man we prepare to honor.

It was not too long ago that Martin painted a vivid picture of what an America united would look like...an America in which all children could grow up to realize their full potential. January 20, 1986 must be seen as a way to reflect that vision, a way to celebrate the life and legacy of a man with a dream for all seasons.

The special recognition accorded Martin by the American people provides a unique opportunity for all Americans to reaffirm their faith in nonviolence at a time when violence in all its ugly forms seems to be a way of life. It also gives Americans a special moment to reaffirm their support for Martin's beloved community and for the values that distinguish our republic in this troubled world.

The commission has chosen "Living the Dream" as its theme for the birthday celebration. We see "Martin's Day"—the third Monday of each year—as:

> . . .a day to celebrate the life and dream of Martin Luther King, Jr.
>
> . . .a day to reaffirm the American ideals of freedom, justice and opportunity for all
>
> . . .a day for love, not hate; for understanding, not anger; for peace, not war
>
> . . .a day for the family to share together, to reach out to relatives and friends and to mend broken relationships

...a day when people of all races, religions, classes and stations in life put aside their differences and join in a spirit of togetherness

...a day for our nation to pay tribute to Martin Luther King, Jr., who awakened in us the best qualities of the American spirit

...a day for nations of the world to cease all violent actions, seek non-violent solutions and demonstrate that peace is not just a dream but a real possibility, if only for one day.

We have come too far to be discouraged or to lose hope or to stop believing in the justice for which he died, if we embrace his dream of a community where we can *all* come to love and care for one another, we will strive to complete his unfinished agenda, we will make his unfinished work our own.

Let us be grateful for the providence that sends among us men and women with the courage and vision to stand peacefully but unyieldingly for what is right. Let us also make this a time when we rededicate ourselves to carry on the work of justice.

Martin showed how much good a single life, well led, can accomplish. Let Americans honor his memory by pledging in their own lives to do everything they can to make America a place where his dream of freedom and brotherhood and sisterhood will grow up and flourish and we can all be proud to sing with new meaning, "From every mountainside, Let freedom ring."

Coretta Scott King, widow of Dr. Martin Luther King, Jr., is chairperson of the Martin Luther King, Jr. Federal Holiday Commission and president of The Martin Luther King, Jr. Center for Nonviolent Social Change, Inc.

Adapted from a copyrighted speech delivered in Washington, D.C. on May 20, 1985

The Courage to Live Life to the Fullest Purpose

"Every now and then I think about my own death, and I think about my own funeral.... I don't want a long funeral. And if you get somebody to deliver the eulogy, tell them not to talk too long.... Tell them not to mention that I have a Nobel Peace

Prize.... Tell them not to mention that I have three or four hundred other awards.... I'd like somebody to mention that day, that Martin Luther King, Jr., tried to give his life serving others. I'd like for somebody to say that day that Martin Luther King, Jr., tried to love somebody....

"Say that I was a drum major for justice. Say that I was a drum major for peace. That I was a drum major for righteousness. And all of the other shallow things will not matter. I won't have any money to leave behind. I won't have the fine and luxurious things of life to leave behind. But I just want to leave a committed life behind."

Reprinted by arrangement with INTELLECTUAL PROPER-TIES MANAGEMENT, ATLANTA, GEORGIA, AS EXCLUSIVE LICENSOR OF THE KING ESTATE

Important Dates in the Life of Dr. Martin Luther King, Jr.

IMPORTANT DATES IN THE LIFE OF MLK

Dr. King as pastor of Dexter Avenue Baptist Church in Montgomery, Ala.

1929

JANUARY 15
Martin Luther King Jr. is second of three children born to the Rev. Martin Luther King Sr. and Mrs. Alberta Christine Williams King in Atlanta.

1935

SEPTEMBER
He enrolls at David T. Howard Elementary School, but later attended Atlanta University Laboratory School. Thereafter he attended Booker T. Washington High School, skipping ninth grade and entering sophomore class.

With Montgomery Bus Boycott heroine Mrs. Rosa Parks

1944

SEPTEMBER
He enters Morehouse College at age 15 after passing entrance examination and skipping 12th grade.

1948

FEBRUARY 25
He is ordained to the Baptist ministry.

JUNE
He graduates, at 19, from Morehouse with bachelor of arts degree in sociology.

SEPTEMBER
He enters Crozer Theological Seminary where he was one of six Black students.

Sitting for mugshot after being arrested for leading Montgomery Bus Boycott

1951

JUNE
With an A average, King is graduated from Crozer, where he was most outstanding student, president of the senior class and recipient of graduate fellowship.

44

With his wife, Coretta, celebrating legal victory which ended boycott

EBONY • January, 1986   **Continued on Page 46**

1953

JUNE 18
He marries Coretta Scott in Marion, Ala. Martin Luther King Sr. officiated.

1954

MAY 17
Racial segregation in public schools is declared unconstitutional by U.S. Supreme Court which ruled unanimously in the *Brown V. Board of Education* case.

SEPTEMBER 1
Dr. King becomes full-time pastor of Dexter Avenue Baptist Church in Montgomery, Ala.

1955

JUNE 5
He is awarded Ph.D. in systematic theology at Boston University.

NOVEMBER 17
The Kings' first child, Yolanda Denise, is born in Montgomery.

DECEMBER 1
Mrs. Rosa Parks is arrested and charged with violating Montgomery city segregation code after refusing to relinquish her bus seat to a White man.

DECEMBER 5
Montgomery Bus Boycott begins.

1956

JANUARY 26
Dr. King is arrested and charged with driving 30 mph in a 25 mph zone in Montgomery. After being jailed for the first time in his life, he is released on his own recognizance.

JANUARY 30
A bomb is thrown onto the porch of Dr. King's Montgomery home while he is away addressing a mass meeting. Mrs. King, their baby, and a visiting friend are not injured. Dr. King calms and disperses the angry crowd that gathers.

FEBRUARY 2
A suit asking that Montgomery's travel segregation laws be declared unconstitutional is filed in federal district court.

FEBRUARY 21
Dr. King and others are indicted in the Montgomery Bus Boycott.

JUNE 4
Racial segregation on city bus lines

Meeting with Vice President and Mrs. Richard M. Nixon in Ghana

Visiting with Indian Prime Minister Jawaharlal Nehru in New Delhi (Feb. 10, 1959)

Arrested by Montgomery police for "loitering" (Sept. 3, 1958)

Receiving first aid after being stabbed in the chest by Izola Curry (Sept. 20, 1958)

EBONY • January, 1986
Continued on Page 48

is ruled unconstitutional by a U.S. District Court.

NOVEMBER 13
The U.S. Supreme Court upholds the decision of the U.S. District Court in declaring unconstitutional Alabama's state and local bus segregation laws.

DECEMBER 21
Montgomery city buses are integrated for the first time.

1957

JANUARY 10-11
He is elected president of the Southern Christian Leadership Conference at founding meeting.

JANUARY 27
An unexploded bomb is found on Dr. King's front porch.

MAY 17
Dr. King delivers the speech, "Give Us The Ballot," at Lincoln Memorial during Prayer Pilgrimage For Freedom on the third anniversary of the U.S. Supreme Court's desegregation decision.

SEPTEMBER
President Dwight D. Eisenhower federalizes the Arkansas National Guard and dispatches paratroopers of the 101st Airborne Division to protect nine Black students who integrated all-White Central High School in Little Rock.

OCTOBER 23
The Kings' second child, Martin Luther III, is born.

1958

SEPTEMBER 3
He is arrested (for third time) and charged with loitering near the Montgomery Recorder's Court. The charge is later changed to "failure to obey an officer" and he is released on $100 bond.

SEPTEMBER 17
Stride Toward Freedom: The Montgomery Story, Dr. King's first book, is published.

SEPTEMBER 20
Izola Curry, later alleged to be mentally deranged, stabs Dr. King while he is autographing his book in Harlem.

1959

FEBRUARY 2-MARCH 10
At the invitation of India's Prime Minister Jawaharlal Nehru, Dr. and Mrs. King spend a month in India

Exchanging quips with presidential candidate John F. Kennedy

studying Gandhi's techniques of nonviolence.

NOVEMBER 29
Dr. King resigns as pastor of Dexter Avenue Baptist Church.

1960

JANUARY 24
He becomes co-pastor, with his father, of Ebenezer Baptist Church in Atlanta.

FEBRUARY 1
Students in Greensboro, N.C., stage the first lunch-counter sit-ins.

FEBRUARY 17
Dr. King is issued an arrest warrant charging perjury in filing his 1956 and 1958 Alabama state taxes.

MAY 28
An all-White jury in Montgomery acquits Dr. King of perjury charge.

OCTOBER 19
In Atlanta, Dr. King and 51 others are arrested for participating in a sit-in and are jailed on charges of violating the state's trespass law.

OCTOBER 22
The Atlanta trespass charges are dropped and all demonstrators are released except Dr. King, who is held on charges of violating a probated sentence in a September, 1960, traffic case. He is transferred to the DeKalb County Jail and then to Reidsville State Prison.

OCTOBER 27
Dr. King is released on $2000 appeal bond after Robert F. Kennedy, campaign manager for presidential candidate John F. Kennedy, intervened.

1961

JANUARY 30

The King's third child, Dexter Scott, is born in Atlanta.

MAY 4
Freedom Riders, organized by CORE to integrate interstate buses, leave Washington, D.C., on a Greyhound bus shortly after the Supreme Court outlaws segregation in interstate transportation. On May 14, racists bomb and burn the bus near Anniston, Ala., and the Riders are attacked in Birmingham. On May 20, a new group of Freedom Riders is assaulted in Montgomery. Attorney General Robert Kennedy sends 400 U.S. marshals to the city to maintain order.

DECEMBER 16
At an Albany demonstration, Dr. King is arrested and charged with obstructing sidewalk and parading without permit.

1962

FEBRUARY 27
At a trial, Dr. King is convicted of leading the Albany march.

JULY 27
At an Albany city hall prayer vigil, Dr. King is arrested and charged with failure to obey a police officer, obstructing the sidewalk and disorderly conduct.

OCTOBER 16
Dr. King meets with President John F. Kennedy at the White House.

1963

MARCH 28
Bernice Albertine, the Kings' fourth child, is born.

APRIL 3
Dr. King opens the Birmingham campaign to protest segregation. On April 12, he, Dr. Abernathy and 53 demonstrators are jailed.

  Continued on Page 50

APRIL 16
Dr. King writes his "Letter From Birmingham Jail" during his imprisonment.

MAY 2
Safety Commissioner Eugene "Bull" Connor orders police to use dogs and fire hoses on Black youth demonstrators.

MAY 20
Birmingham's segregation ordinances are ruled unconstitutional by the U.S. Supreme Court.

JUNE 12
Medgar Evers, a Jackson, Miss., NAACP leader, is assassinated before dawn by a rifle bullet at his home.

AUGUST 28
The largest integrated mass protest, The March On Washington, is held. Dr. King delivers his "I Have A Dream" speech before 250,000 at the Lincoln Memorial.

SEPTEMBER
Strength To Love, Dr. King's fourth book, is published.

SEPTEMBER 15
Four children attending Sunday School at the Sixteenth Street Baptist Church in Birmingham are killed and 21 others are injured when the church is bombed.

NOVEMBER 22
President John F. Kennedy is assassinated in Dallas.

1964

JUNE
Dr. King's fifth book, *Why We Can't Wait*, is published.

JUNE
At Soldier Field in Chicago, Dr. King addresses 75,000 persons at a civil rights rally organized by an interracial, interfaith citizens group.

JUNE 11
With Rev. Abernathy and a party of 16, Dr. King stages a sit-in at an exclusive restaurant in St. Augustine, Fla. Dr. King is arrested for the 12th time and charged with violating Florida's "unwanted guest law."

JUNE 21
Three civil rights workers (James Chaney, Black, and Andrew Goodman and Michael Schwerner, both White) are reported missing after traveling to Philadelphia, Miss.

Addressing 1963 March on Washington crowd

Meeting with President Johnson and (l. to r.) Roy Wilkins, James Farmer and Whitney Young at the White House

With Rev. Abernathy during audience with Pope Paul VI and Monsignor Paul Marcinkus at the Vatican

JULY 2
Dr. King is present at the signing of the Civil Rights Act of 1964, by President Lyndon B. Johnson at the White House. The bill, which guaranteed access to public accommodations, was submitted to Congress by President Kennedy.

JULY 18-23
A Black man is killed during race riots in Harlem.

AUGUST 4
FBI agents discover bodies of James Chaney, Andrew Goodman and Michael Schwerner buried near Philadelphia, Miss.

SEPTEMBER 18
At the Vatican, Dr. King has an audience with Pope Paul VI.

DECEMBER 10
In Oslo, Norway, Dr. King receives the Nobel Peace Prize.

1965

FEBRUARY 21
Malcolm X is assassinated at Audubon Ballroom in New York City.

50

Continued on Page 52

MARCH 7
SNCC and SCLC demonstrators led by John Lewis and Hosea Williams are beaten by state troopers and sheriff deputies when they attempt to cross a bridge during a Montgomery to Selma march. Alabama Governor George Wallace had prohibited the march.

MARCH 9
Civil rights worker Rev. James Reeb, a White Unitarian minister from Cleveland, is beaten by four White men in Selma. He dies two days later.

Receiving the Nobel Peace Prize in Oslo, Norway (Dec. 10, 1964)

MARCH 15
President Johnson addresses a joint session of Congress to call for passage of the Voting Rights Bill, using the Civil Rights Movement slogan "We Shall Overcome."

MARCH 21-25
Protected by federal troops, more than 3,000 civil rights marchers leave Selma for Montgomery. Along the way they are joined by 25,000 marchers, and on reaching the Alabama State Capitol are addressed by Dr. King.

Leading march in Mississippi flanked by Andrew Young, Floyd McKissick, Stokley Carmichael

MARCH 25
The wife of a Detroit Teamsters Union business agent, Mrs. Viola Liuzzo, is shot and killed while driving to Selma after the rally.

JULY
During visit by Dr. King to Chicago, SCLC joins with the Coordinating Council of Community Organizations, led by Al Raby.

AUGUST–DECEMBER
Dr. King and SCLC spearhead voter registration campaigns in Greene, Wilcox and Eutaw counties in Alabama, and in the cities of Montgomery and Birmingham.

AUGUST 6
President Johnson signs the 1965 Voting Rights Act.

At Montgomery march with (l. to r.) Mrs. Rosa Parks, Rev. and Mrs. Ralph Abernathy, and Mrs. King

AUGUST 11-16
Thirty-five persons, including 28 Blacks, are killed during riots in the Los Angeles' Watts neighborhood.

1966

FEBRUARY
Dr. King moves into an inner city neighborhood on Chicago's West Side.

MAY 16
At a large Washington rally to protest the Vietnam War, an antiwar statement by Dr. King is read.

JUNE 6
Activist James Meredith is shot af-

Announcing open housing campaign at a Chicago press conference with (l. to r.) James Bevel and Al Raby

ter starting a 220-mile "March Against Fear" from Memphis to Jackson, Miss. Dr. King, Floyd McKissick and others continued the March. For the first time, Stokely Carmichael and Willie Ricks use the "Black Power" slogan.

JULY 10
Dr. King launches a campaign to integrate housing in Chicago.

AUGUST 5
Leading march through Chicago's Gage Park area, Dr. King is stoned by angry Whites.

1967

JANUARY
Dr. King completes his sixth book, *Where Do We Go From Here?*

JULY 12-17
During rebellions in Newark, N.J., 23 persons are killed and 725 are injured.

JULY 23-30
In the worse race riots of the century, 43 persons die and 324 are injured in Detroit.

JULY 26
Dr. King, A. Philip Randolph, Roy Wilkins and Whitney Young call for rebellions to end, terming them "ineffective and damaging to the civil rights cause..."

OCTOBER 30
U.S. Supreme Court upholds the contempt-of-court convictions of Dr. King and seven others who led 1963 marches in Birmingham. They serve four-day jail sentences.

NOVEMBER 27
Dr. King announces SCLC's "Poor People's Campaign."

1968

MARCH 28
Dr. King leads 6,000 civil rights protestors on a march through downtown Memphis in support of sanitation workers' strike. Against his wishes, disorder breaks out. One 16-year-old is killed and 50 persons are injured.

APRIL 3
At the Memphis Masonic Temple, Dr. King delivers the speech, "I've Been To The Mountaintop."

APRIL 4
As he stands talking on the balcony of the Lorraine Motel in Memphis, Dr. King is shot in the neck by a sniper and dies at St. Joseph's Hospital. James Earl Ray is later convicted for the murder.

54

Leading march in Memphis flanked by Rev. R. H. Jackson and Rev. Abernathy

With aides (l. to r.) Rev. Hosea Williams, Rev. Jesse Jackson, and Rev. Abernathy at the Lorraine Motel in Memphis the day before assassination

Lying mortally shot on balcony of Lorraine Motel while aides point toward direction of shots

Viewed for last time by his widow and children (l. to r.) Yolanda, Bernice, Martin III and Dexter.

Educational Resources for
Golden Literary Treasury

The Day of Days, December 5

I.   Knowing Why Choose the item or items that best complete the statement.

1.   Rev. Martin L. King, Jr. had gotten up at 5:30 a.m. to:
a) prepare himself for work
b) get an airplane flight to Atlanta
c) see how many people were riding the bus

2.   The bus line that ran past Rev. King's house was:
a) The Grey Line
b) The South Jackson Line
c) The Blue Goose Line

3.   Coretta called, "Martin, Martin, come quickly" because she:
a) did not want him to miss the bus
b) wanted him to witness the crowded bus
c) wanted him to see that the bus was almost empty

4.   The South Jackson Line largest passengers were:
a) wealthy whites who did not wish to drive
b) domestic workers going to their jobs
c) soldiers from the air base

5.   The first bus ran on the South Jackson Line about;
a) 5:30 a.m.
b) 6:00 a.m.
c) 7:00 a.m.

6. To maintain the boycott in Montgomery, the protesters used:
   a) car pools and mules
   b) buses and cars
   c) trains and subways

7. Why did Rev. King go to the crowded police court around 9:30 a.m.?
   a) He was charged with organizing the boy-cott
   b) He was the defendant for Rosa Parks
   c) He was attending the trial of Rosa Parks

8. The court council for Rosa Parks was:
   a) Ralph Abernathy
   b) Martin L. King
   c) Fred D. Gray

9. The court in Montgomery, Alabama found Rosa Parks guilty of disobeying the segregation law and fined her:
   a) Ten dollars
   b) Fourteen dollars
   c) Twenty dollars

10. The conviction of Rosa Parks had a two-told impact:
    a) It motivated blacks to positive action and it put the segregation law on trial to test its validity.
    b) It served to warn the black community to obey segregation laws and to shun protesters.
    c) It taught the black community to be satisfied and to wait for justice.

11. The role of the Montgomery ad hoc committee was to:
    a) unite people for a specific purpose
    b) call people together for an athletic game
    c) bring people together for a cross country trip

12. What was the purpose of the mass meeting?
    a) to celebrate a united church convention
    b) to provide a scholarship drive for Alabama State College
    c) to institute an official plan for the boycott to end segregation on buses

13. The mass meeting was called together by:
    a) E. D. Nixon
    b) Roy Bennett
    c) Rufus Lewis

14. What pastor is paired with the correct church?
    a) Rev. Martin L. King and Dexter Avenue Baptist Church
    b) Rev. U. F. Fields and Beulah Baptist Church
    c) Rev. W. F. Alford and Bell Street Baptist Church

15. The man who read the resolutions to boycott the bus was:
    a) E.D. Nixon
    b) Ralph Abernathy
    c) Fred D. Gray

16. Which one of these organizations seek to improve the lives of black people?
    a) White Citizen's Council
    b) NAACP
    c) Ku Klux Klan

17. The statement, "Let your conscience be your guide," means:
    a) Use your Christian belief to guide you to do what is right
    b) Be free and do what you want to do whether right or wrong.
    c) Be free to look out just for yourself—never mind others.

18. "Let no man pull you so low as to make you hate him," is a quote from which person?
    a) Martin L. King
    b) Rosa Parks
    c) Booker T. Washington

19. Rosa Parks introduced at the mass meeting by:
    a) Ralph Abernathy
    b) E. N. French
    c) Martin L. King

20. The victory of the mass meeting revealed:
    a) a new sense of dignity and destiny for black people
    b) an unsuccessful organization
    c) a boycott that lacked planning

TESTING CRITICAL THINKING SKILLS

I. Review the reading of **The Day of Days, December 5,** explain the meaning of E. D. Nixon's statement:

> We are acting like little boys.

II. In your own words discuss the decision that E. D. Nixon challenged the people to make in the statement below and explain the choices that were before them:

> We'd better decide now if we are going to be fearless men or scared boys.

III. In your own words explain the meaning and pattern of thought in the statement below:

> Would it not be better to call off the protest while it is still a success rather than let it go on a few more days and fizzle out? We have already proved our united strength to the white community. If we stop now we can get anything we want from the bus company, simply because they will have the feeling that we can do it again. But if we continue, and most of the people return to the buses tomorrow or the next day, the white people will laugh at us, and we will end up getting nothing.

The Day of Days, December 5
Martin L. King, Jr.

IDENTIFY the following persons by matching them with the correct statement. Write the alphabet of your choice in the blank provided.

Column A

_____   1. Fred D. Gray

_____   2. Roy Bennett

_____   3. E. D. Nixon

_____   4. Dr. Wilson

_____   5. Rev. W. L. Alford

_____   6. Rev. U. J. Fields

_____   7. E. N. French

_____   8. Ralph Abernathy

_____   9. Coretta S. King

_____   10. Dr. Martin L. King, Jr.

_____   11. Rufus Lewis

_____   12. Rosa Parks

Column B

a. called the people together for the first evening mass meeting of the boycott

b. Pastor of the church where mass meeting was held

c. chief council for the boycott movement who defended Rosa Parks

d. President of the NAACP

e. Minister of Bell Street Baptist Church

f. introduced Rosa Parks at the mass meeting

g. Minister of Beulah Baptist Church

h. woman who refused to give her seat to a white man

i. elected leader of the bus boycott

j. wife of Dr. Martin L. King

k. assistant to Dr. M. L. King

l. nominated Dr. King for president at mass meeting

Addendum

SUGGESTED CLASSROOM ACTIVITIES

for

THE MONTGOMERY BUS BOYCOTT

SCIENCE

A. Vocabulary

    1. bomb (advantages and disadvantages)

    2. explode (danger)

    3. smoke (aftermath)

    4. fingerprint (unique to each person)

B. Concepts

    1. The discovery of the bomb has become both a threat and a menace to mankind.

    2. The particles released from a bomb may affect the population of a people for many decades to come.

MATHEMATICS

A. Vocabulary

    1. mile
    2. thousand
    3. expensive
    4. check (money)
    5. contribution
    6. account (checking and savings)
    7. finance

B. Word Problems

    1. There were 17,500 black bus riders in Montgomery, Alabama. The bus boycott was 98% effective. Approximately how many black people rode the bus during the boycott?

    2. Some middle-age people walked during the boycott instead of riding in car pools as a symbolic act. If one person walked 12 miles each day for 5 days a week, how many miles could this person walk in 12 months?

    3. It took as much as five thousand dollars to run the bus boycott each month. What was the expense of running this boycott each day? What was the cost for running the boycott for 12 months?

SOCIAL STUDIES

A. Vocabulary

1. segregation
2. integration
3. desegregation
4. picketing
5. protest
6. boycott

7. civil rights
8. discrimination
9. organization
10. route
11. unity
12. crusader
13. non-violent
14. amendment
(14th)

15. constitution
16. bail
17. **author provide**
18. second-class citizens
19. car pool
20. persuade

B. Concepts

1. "An injustice anywhere is a threat to justice everywhere."

2. Automation and technology have made it possible to bring countries of the world closer together in social relationships (contributions from Tokyo, Switzerland and Singapore).

3. A common goal may sometimes unite people.

ENGLISH

A. Things to Do

1. Dramatize scenes from the life of Dr. Martin L. King, Jr.

2. Write a poem or composition about the non-violent crusader.

3. Write a book report on the life of Dr. King.

4. Prepare a newsreel on the national celebration of Dr. Martin L. King's birthday.

B. Debates

    1. Compare the views of Dr. King with those of Malcolm X.

    2. When Dr. King spoke out against the Vietnam War, was he still presenting himself as a non-violent crusader?

C. Topics for Discussion

    1. Dr. King effectuated changes in the life of black people in the South and the North.

    2. Dr. King made it possible for many blacks to be elected to high positions in local, state, and the national government (U.S. Representatives, mayors, and judges).

    3. Dr. King refused to live in the affluent black community in Atlanta, Georgia, instead he lived in one of the poorest sections.

ART

A. Group Work

    1. Do a mural on the "March On Washington," scene.

    2. Make a collage of "The Montgomery Bus Boycott."

B. Individual Work

    1. Sketch pictures of the participants (King, Abernathy, etc.)

    2. Prepare a bulletin board or other displays on the protests and marches led by Dr. King.

RESOURCES

King, C. *My Life with Martin Luther King*. Holt, 1969

King, M. *Stride Toward Freedom*. Harper, 1958

King, M. *Trumpet of Conscience*. Harper, 1968

King, M. *Where Do We Go From Here?* Harper, 1967

King, M. *Why We Can't Wait*. Harper, 1964

"From Booker T. To Martin Luther King" Ebony, Nov. '62
"I've Been To The Mountaintop" Ebony, May '68

Conyers' King bill finally wins after 15-year struggle

By KEN FIREMAN
Free Press Politics Writer

WASHINGTON—When U.S. Rep. John Conyers introduced legislation to make the Rev. Martin Luther King's birthday a national holiday, four days after the civil-rights leader was murdered on April 4, 1968, the reaction in Congress was a collective yawn.

"It was considered just the tossing of a legislative bouquet to Martin Luther King," the Detroit Democrat recalled Friday. "It wasn't taken very seriously. It didn't get anywhere. No hearings were held, and I can't even remember if it was introduced over in the Senate."

But Conyers persevered, reintroducing the bill each time a new Congress convened. And last week, after 15 years, Conyers and his allies celebrated victory when the Senate—after acrimonious debate—overwhelmingly approved the legislation.

The House already has approved the bill, which will make the third Monday in January a national holiday in King's honor, beginning in 1986. President Reagan, who initially opposed it, has promised to sign it into law..

The legislation, which Conyers said was his first major bill to be enacted since he entered Congress in 1965, prevailed over the opposition of Sen. Jesse Helms, R-N.C.

Helms argued that Dr. King was unworthy of the honor because the civil-rights leader had associated with communists and subversives during the years he led the Southern Christian Leadership Conference. Helms went to court in an unsuccessful bid to unseal government files compiled on King's activities by the FBI during the 1960s.

But Conyers said Helms' tactics were so heavy-handed that he embarrassed many uncommitted senators and therefore increased support for the legislation.

"He unwittingly contributed to cementing the success of the bill," Conyers said. "He made it pretty hard to identify with him. He made himself an outcast."

BESIDES HELMS' unintended assistance, Conyers attributed the success of the bill to:

- The growing political clout of black voters in many states, which led many previously unsympathetic congressmen and senators to conclude that it would be politically wise to vote for the legislation.
- The fact that many states, counties and municipalities—including Michigan, Wayne County and Detroit—already have declared King's birthday a holiday.

• "A genuine feeling...that there ought to be some sort of honor for Dr. King, that the man deserved it."

CONYERS acknowledges that some of his colleagues voted for the bill for less-than-altruistic reasons. But he finds it encouraging that some congressmen and senators now find it politically expedient to honor King.

"I'd be the first to concede that opportunism, pressure, fear of defeat...enters into a how a person votes," he said. "But that's a measure of black empowerment. The sad thing is that they never had to do that (support the King bill) before."

Reagan initially opposed the bill on the ground that adding another national holiday would be too costly to the federal budget and the national economy. He eventually changed his mind, saying he was persuaded that the symbolism of honoring King outweighed his objections.

But Conyers feels politics played a large role in Reagan's reversal.

"To have such strong bipartisan support in both houses and to have him (Reagan) veto it would have been very damaging politically to him," Conyers said.

THE FIRST inkling Conyers had that Reagan might sign the bill came Jan. 15, when the president held a large reception in the White House to mark Dr. King's birthday. Ironically, in Conyers' view, Reagan was the first president to so honor King.

"It's very strange," he said. "When (Jimmy) Carter was here I couldn't get this thing going. Now, with Reagan and a Republican Senate, we get it passed."

Conyers' efforts were aided by Motown singer Stevie Wonder, who campaigned for the bill at rallies and recorded a song, "Happy Birthday," to promote a King national holiday.

Conyers acknowledges that making King's birthday a national holiday is a largely symbolic gesture. But he says he believes it will have a salutory effect on the nation's racial divisions.

(Reprinted with permission of the Detroit Free Press)

SUBJECT GUIDE TO BOOKS IN PRINT ON MARTIN LUTHER KING, JR.

Alico, Stella H. *Benjamin Franklin-Martin Luther King, Jr.* (Pendulum Illustrated Biography Ser.) (Illus.). (gr. 4-12). 1979, text ed. 5.00 (ISBN 0-8830)-367-7); pap. text ed. 1.95 (ISBN 0-88301-353-3); wkbk 1.25 (ISBN 8-88301-377-0). Pendulum Pr.

Bennett, Lerone, Jr. *What Manner of Man: A Biography of Martin Luther King, Jr.*, 1929-1968. 9.95 (ISBN 0-87485-027.4) Johnson Chi.

Crawford, Fred R., et al. *Certain Reactions by the Atlanta Public to the Death of the Rev. Dr. Martin Luther King, Jr.* LC 73-85669. 1969. pap. 3.00 (ISBN 0-89937-023-3). Ctr Res Soc Chg.

Davis, Lenwood G. *I Have a Dream: The Life & Times of Martin Luther King, Jr.* LC 70-154202. 303p. 1973. Repr. of 1969 ed. lib. bdg. 17.00x (ISBN 0-8371-5977-6, DHD&), Greenwood.

Ebony Editors, *Martin Luther King, Jr.* (Ebony Picture Biography Ser.). (Illus., Orig.). 1968. pap. 1.50 (ISBN 0-87485-025.8). Johnson Chi.

Fisher, William H. *Free at Last: A Bibliography of Martin Luther King, Jr.* LC 77-22202. 1977. 10.00 (ISBN 0-8108-1081-6). Scarecrow

Garrow, David J. *The FBI and Martin Luther King Jr.* 1981. 15.95 (ISBN 0-393-01509-2). Norton.

Hoyt, Robert G. *Martin Luther King, Jr.* LC 70-124086. (Illus.). 1970. 9.95 (ISBN 0-87294-028-4). Country Beautiful.

Lewis, David L. *King: A Biography.* 2nd ed. (Blacks in the New York Ser.). 1978. 17.50 (ISBN 0-25200679-8); pap. 5.95 (ISBN 0-252-00680-1). Univ. of Ill. Pr.

Lincoln, C. Eric. *Martin Luther King, Jr.: A Profile.* LC 69-16828. (American Profiles Ser.). 232 p. 1969 pap. 4.95 (ISBN 0-8090-0209-4). Hill & Wang.

Lomax, Louis. *To Kill a Black Man.* LC 68-8400. (Orig.). 1968. pap. 0.95 (ISBN 0-87067-160-X, BH160). Holloway.

Luther, Martin & Kepler, Thomas S., eds. *Table Talk of Martin Luther.* (Summit Bks.). 1979. pap. 3.95 (ISBN 0-8010-5408-7). Baker Bk.

McKnight, Janet, ed. *Three Assassinations: The Deaths of John & Robert Kennedy & Martin Luther King.* LC 77-154630. (Illus.). 1971. Repr. 17.50x ISBN 0-87196-190-3). Facts on File.

Newton, Michael. *A Case of Conspiracy.* (Orig.). 1980. pap. 2.25 (ISBN 0-87067-003-4, BH003). Holloway.

Paris, Peter J. *Black Leaders in Conflict: Joseph H. Jackson,* Martin Luther King, Jr., Malcolm X. Adam Clayton Powell Jr. LC 78-3833, 1978. pap. 6.95 (ISBN 0-8298-0336-X). Pilgrim, N.Y.

Philosophy of Non-Violence: Martin Luther King-Mini-Play. (People of Conscience Ser.) (gr. 8 up) 1978. 3.00 (ISBN 0-89550-313-1).

Schulke, Flip, ed. *Martin Luther King, Jr. A Documentary... Montgomery to Memphis.* (Illus.) 224 p. 1976. 19.95 (ISBN 0-393-07487-0); limited ed. o.p. 100.00 (ISBN 0-685-62030-1); pap. 9.95 (ISBN 0-393-07492-7). Norton.

Scruggs, Julius R. *Baptist Preachers with Social Consciousness: A Comparative Study of Martin Luther King Jr. & Harry Emerson Fosdick.* 72 p. 1979. 5.00 (ISBN 0-8059-2501-5). Dorrance.

Smith, Ervin. *The Ethics of Martin Luther King, Jr.* (Studies in American Religion: Vol. 2). 1982 soft cover 24.95x (ISBN 0-88946-974-1). E. Mellen.

Smith, Kenneth L. & Zepp, Ira G., Jr. *Search for the Beloved Community: The Thinking of Martin Luther King, Jr.* LC 73-10777. 160p. 1974. 6.95 (ISBN 0-8170-0611-7). Judson.

Spruill, Robert. *Death & Life of Dr. Martin Luther King, Jr.* 1980. 4.00 (ISBN 0-8062-1174-1). Carlton.

Walton, Hanes, Jr. *Political Philosophy of Martin Luther King, Jr.* LC 76-11260. (Contributions in Afro-American & African Studies: No. 10). 1971. text. ed. 13.95 (ISBN 0-8371-4661-5); pap. 4.95 (ISBN 0-8371-8913-4).

Weisburg, Harold. *Frame-up: The Martin Luther King-James Earl Ray. Case.* LC 70-149057. 10.00x (ISBN 0-911606-06-8). Weisburg.

Wilson, Beth P. *Giants for Justice: Bethune, Randolph & King.* LC 77-88971 (gr. 5 up). 1978. 6.95 (ISBN 0-15-230781-8, HJ). Harbrace J.

Wofford, Harris. *Of Kennedys & Kings: Making Sense of the Sixties.* 496p. 1980. 17.50 (ISBN 0-374-22432-3). FS&G.

JUVENILE LITERATURE ON DR. MARTIN LUTHER KING, JR.

Behrens, June. Martin Luther King, Jr. *The Story of a Dream.* (Holiday Play Bks.) (Ills.) (gr. k-4) PLB 8.65 (ISBN 0-516-08879-3, Golden Gat). Childrens.

Clayton, Ed. *Martin Luther King: The Peaceful Warrior.* (gr. 4-6). 1969. pap. 1.50 (ISBN 0-671-29932-8). PB.

DeKay, James T. *Meet Martin Luther King Jr.* LC 78-79789. (Step-up Books Ser.) (gr. 3-6) 1969. 3.95 (ISBN (0-394-80055-9, BYR); PLB 4.99 (ISBN 0-394-90055-3). Random.

Faber, Doris & Faber, Howard. *The Assassination of Martin Luther King, Jr.* LC 78-1726. (Focus Bks.) (Illus.) 1978. lib. bdg. 6.90 S&l (ISBN 0-531-02465-2). Watts.

Haskins, James. *The Life & Death of Martin Luther King, Jr.* LC 77-3157 (Illus.) (gr. 5 up) 1977. PLB. 6.96 (ISBN 0-688-51802-8). Lothrop.

Martin Luther King Jr: Mini-Play. (Black American Ser.) (gr. 5 up). 1977. 3.00 (ISBN 0-89550-363.8). RIM.

Patterson, Lillie. *Martin Luther King, Jr: Man of Peace.* LC69-19152 (American All Ser.). (Illus.) (gr. 3-6) 1969. PLB 6.95 (ISBN 0-8116-4555-x). Garrard.

Preston, Edward. *Martin Luther King: Fighter for Freedom.* LC 68-8391 (gr. 7-8). 1970. 5.95 (ISBN 0-385-08923-6). Doubleday.

Wilson, Beth P. *Martin Luther King, Jr.* (See & Read Biographies) (Illus.) (gr. K-3). 1971. PLB 5.99 (ISBN 0-399-60452-9). Putnam.

Young, Margaret B. *Picture Life of Martin Luther King, Jr.* LC 67-20866. (Picture Life Bks). (Illus.) (gr. k-3). 1968. PLB 7.40 (ISBN 0-531-00981-5). Watts.

Films and Audio Visual Aids

MARTIN LUTHER KING: FROM MONTGOMERY TO MEMPHIS

This documentary film traces the milestones in the career of this martyr of the civil rights struggle, his role in altering civil rights legislation, and his impact on America from 1954, when he spearheaded the Montgomery, Alabama bus boycott, until his assassination in 1968 in Memphis, Tennessee.

27 minutes Available from: Anti-Defamation League of B'nai B'rith

I HAVE A DREAM (1968)

A biography of Dr. Martin Luther King, Jr. highlighting his major accomplishments. Film leads up to Dr. King's assassination in 1968.

35 minutes Available from: Churchill Films 662 N. Robertson Blvd. Los Angeles, California 90069

LEGACY OF A DREAM (1981, revised 1983)

This film, produced by the Martin Luther King, Jr. Foundation, summarizes Dr. King's accomplishments and provides an overview of his life.

| 26 minutes, color | Available from: | Films Incorporated 440 Park Avenue, S. New York, New York 10016 |

BLACK HISTORY: LOST, STOLEN, OR STRAYED

Bill Cosby narrates this CBS-TV Emmy Award-winning film which returns some of the missing pages of black history to our textbooks. A brief survey of individuals and their contributions and a comparison between African art and its influence on 20th century Western artists point out that black history and culture have been almost totally neglected. The final segment concerns what black communities are doing to erase the stereotyped view and build a positive self-image.

| 40 minutes | Available from: | Anti-Defamation League of B'nai B'rith 823 United Nations Plaza New York, New York 10017 |

MARTIN LUTHER KING: THE MAN AND THE MARCH

This documentary presents an overview of the 1968 Poor People's March on Washington, DC. It deals with Martin Luther King, Jr.'s efforts to organize the march and his ability to understand the need for dignity for everyone.

83 minutes   Available from: University. of
California
Extension Media
  Center
Berkeley, California
94720
(415:642-0460)

MARTIN LUTHER KING, JR.: MAN OF PEACE

This film reviews some of the major events of Martin Luther King, Jr.'s career. It concludes with an interview with Dr. King in which he states our obligation to resist and overcome all injustice in a non-violent way.

30 minutes   Available from: Syracuse University
Film Rental Center
1455 East Colvin St.
Syracuse, New York
13210
(315:479-6631)

BLACK ODYSSEY: A HISTORY OF THE AMERICAN NEGRO—Filmstrip

A unique teaching aid—combining art work, integrated on-screen captions, and a structured teachers' guide—which illustrates the decisive roles played by black men and women during 400 years of American history.

PART I: 16TH CENTURY TO THE CIVIL WAR.

57 frames/black and white/with captions

Black participation in New World exploration; beginnings of the slave trade; the struggle for independence and the spread of slavery; rebellion and escape; the cry for Abolition.

PART II: THE CIVIL WAR TO THE PRESENT

61 frames/black and white/with captions

Civil War and Emancipation; Reconstruction; a reign of terror; early civil rights strides; segregation in two World Wards; successes in the battle for equal rights; the prospects for the future.

Available from Anti-Defamation League of B'nai B'rith

BLACK ODYSSEY KIT

Complete *Black Odyssey* filmstrip and the following supplementary material: 5 copies of *The Record*; 1 copy of *Teacher's Guide to*

American Negro History, by William Loren Katz.

Available from: Anti-Defamation League to B'nai B'rith

BLACK AMERICAN, CIVIL RIGHTS LEADERS: A MULTIMEDIA KIT.

Complete program includes 5 filmstrips, 5 records, 5 portraits, manual guide, and 150 student workbooks. Grade 5 and up. Civil Rights leaders included: Malcolm X, Marcus Garvey, Martin Luther King, Jr., Stokley Carmichael, and W.E.B. DuBois. 1971.

Available from: McGraw Hill Book Company
                       1221 Avenue of the Americas
                       New York, New York 10020
                       (212:997-1221)

WE SHALL OVERCOME

Documentary of the March on Washington, DC, August 28, 1963. Record includes full text of Dr. Martin Luther King, Jr.'s speech, "I Have a Dream."

Available from: Folkways Records
                       43 West 61 Street
                       New York, New York 10023
                       (212:586-7260)